NNAT

Naglieri Nonverbal Ability Test®

SPATIAL

VISUALIZATION

A step by step STUDY GUIDE

GRADE 3

by MindMine

1

Why this book?

Cognitive abilities are brain-based skills related with the mechanisms of learning, memorizing, and paying attention rather than actual knowledge that was learned. **The more you practice, the more you develop** your cognitive flexibility.

- This book is designed to teach concepts and skills in a way kids understand with ease.

- Concepts are taught step by step and introduced incrementally.

- The focus of this book is to provide a solid foundation to fundamental skills. All the skills taught in the book will collectively increase the knowledge and will help kids to prepare and take the test confidently.

- Practice tests that are available in the market may not provide all the concepts needed. This book is aimed to give both concepts and practice.

Who should buy this book?

- 3rd graders taking NNAT test (NNAT2)

- 2nd graders planning to take NNAT (Any Form)

- 1st, 2nd and 3rd graders seeking to enrich their Nonverbal reasoning and Problem-solving skills

📚 What is covered?

This book extensively covers **SPATIAL VISUALIZATION** section of **NNAT Test** with 300 unique questions and 500 secondary questions.

📚 **2 FULL LENGTH PRACTICE TESTS with Answers**

Full Length Practice Test#1	15 Questions
Full Length Practice Test#2	15 Questions

📚 **FUNDAMENTAL CONCEPTS**

📚 **SPATIAL VISUALIZATION QUESTIONS**   300 Questions

📚 **ANSWERS**

📚 Table of Contents

Concept	Page#

5

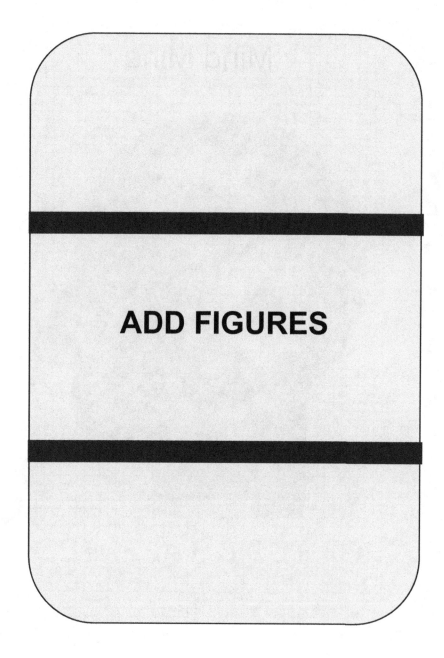

ADD FIGURES

SPATIAL VISUALIZATION

Question

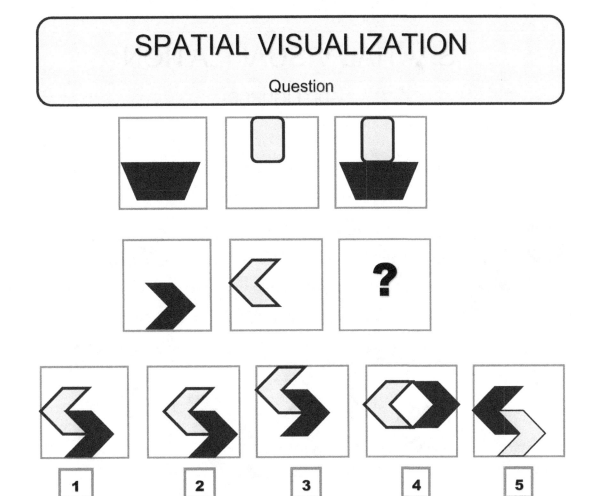

ANSWER: 1

7

SPATIAL VISUALIZATION

ADD FIGURES

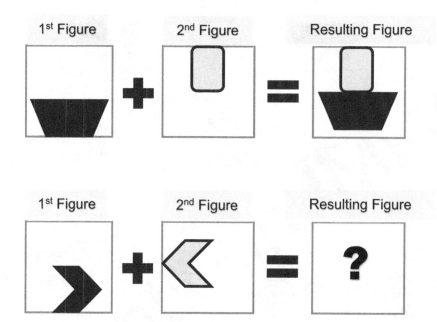

How to solve?

STEP-1: Understand position of figure in 1st Box

Understand position of figure in 2nd Box

STEP-2: Place 1st Figure over 2nd Figure

(or)

Place 2nd Figure over 1st Figure

NOTE: Pay attention to position of each figure in 3rd box. Position of each figure **MUST** match with position of figures in 1st and 2nd boxes.

STEP-3: Find the correct Answer

SPATIAL VISUALIZATION

ADD FIGURES

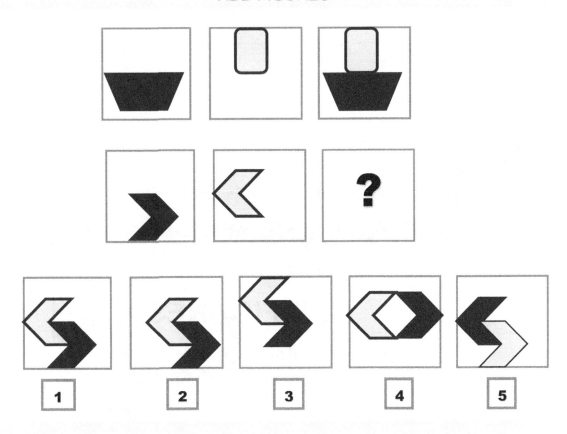

How to solve?

Place 1st Figure over 2nd Figure (or)

Place 2nd Figure over 1st Figure

ANSWER: 1

Answer Choice 2 is incorrect. Gray Arrow is not starting from the left

Answer Choice 3 is incorrect. Gray Arrow Should not touch the top

Answer Choice 4 is incorrect. Black Arrow is not starting from the bottom

Answer Choice 5 is incorrect. Arrow colors are incorrect

9

ADD FIGURES

(Place 2nd figure over 1st figure)

SPATIAL VISUALIZATION

Question

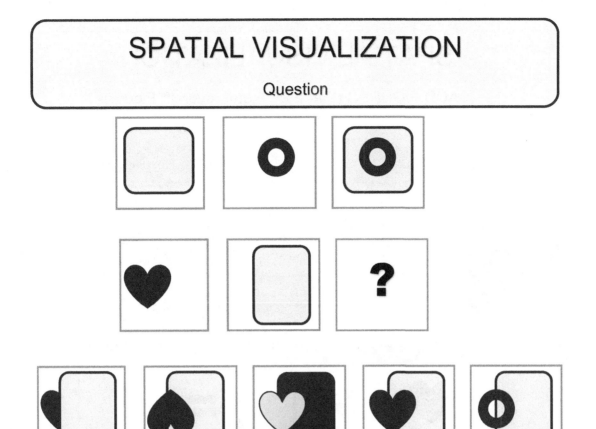

ANSWER: 1

11

SPATIAL VISUALIZATION

ADD FIGURES (Place 2ⁿᵈ Figure over 1ˢᵗ Figure)

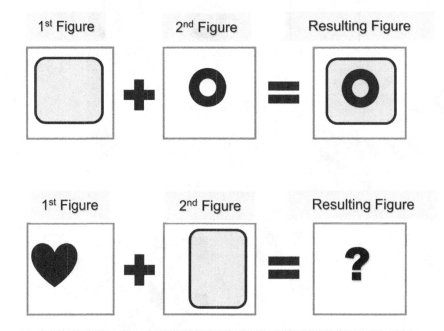

How to solve?

STEP-1: Understand position of figure in 1ˢᵗ Box

Understand position of figure in 2ⁿᵈ Box

STEP-2: *Place 2ⁿᵈ figure over 1ˢᵗ figure*

NOTE: Pay attention to position of each figure in 3ʳᵈ box. Position of each figure **<u>MUST</u>** match with position of figures in 1ˢᵗ and 2ⁿᵈ boxes.

STEP-3: Find the correct Answer

SPATIAL VISUALIZATION

ADD FIGURES (Place 2nd figure over 1st figure)

How to solve?

Place 2nd figure over 1st figure

ANSWER: 1

Answer Choice 2 is incorrect. Gray Heart is flipped

Answer Choice 3 is incorrect. Colors are incorrect

Answer Choice 4 is incorrect. 1st figure is placed on 2nd figure

Answer Choice 5 is incorrect. Heart shape is missing. Circle is incorrect shape.

13

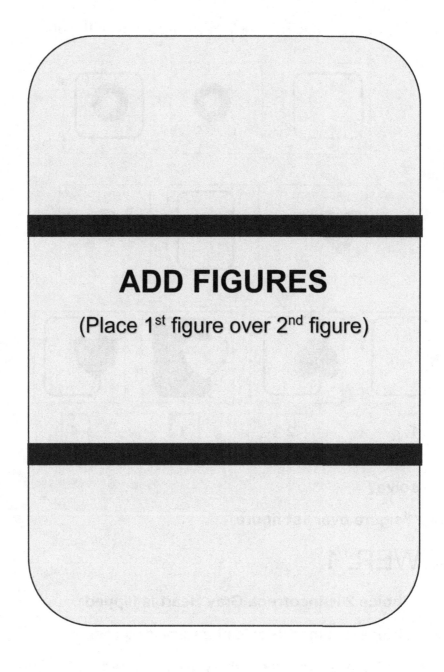

ADD FIGURES

(Place 1st figure over 2nd figure)

SPATIAL VISUALIZATION

Question

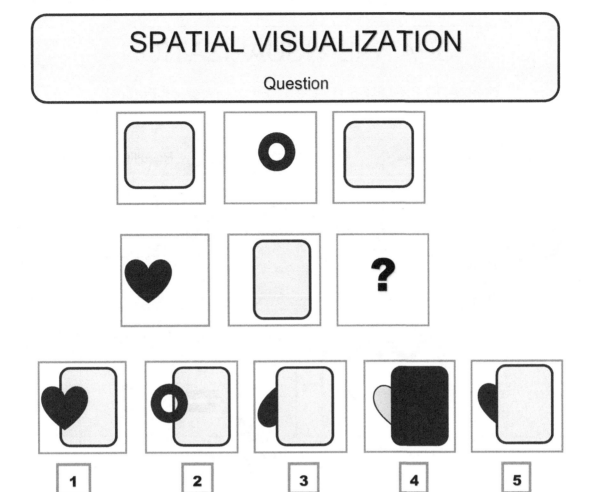

ANSWER: 1

15

SPATIAL VISUALIZATION

ADD FIGURES (Place 1st Figure over 2nd Figure)

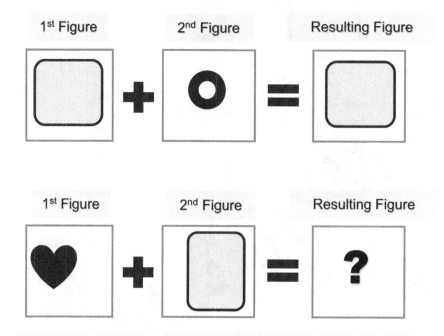

How to solve?

STEP-1: Understand position of figure in 1st Box

Understand position of figure in 2nd Box

STEP-2: *Place 1st figure over 2nd figure*

NOTE: Pay attention to position of each figure in 3rd box. Position of each figure **MUST** match with position of figures in 1st and 2nd boxes.

STEP-3: Find the correct Answer

SPATIAL VISUALIZATION

ADD FIGURES (Place 1st figure over 2nd figure)

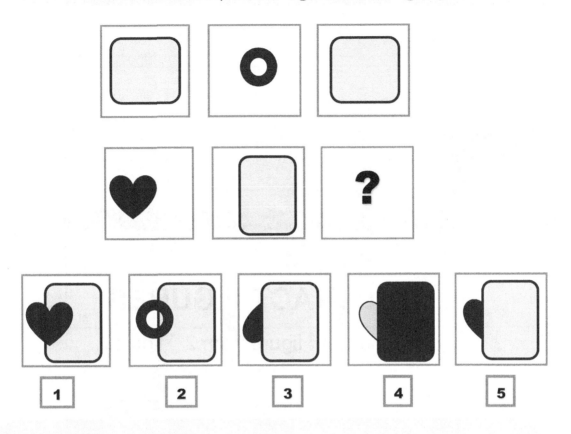

How to solve?

Place 1st figure over 2nd figure

ANSWER: 1

Answer Choice 2 is incorrect. Heart shape is missing. Black circle is incorrect

Answer Choice 3 is incorrect. Heart Shape is flipped. 2nd figure is placed over 1st figure.

Answer Choice 4 is incorrect. Colors are incorrect.

Answer Choice 5 is incorrect. 2nd figure is placed over 1st figure.

SUBTRACT FIGURES

(Remove 1st figure from 2nd figure)

SPATIAL VISUALIZATION

Question

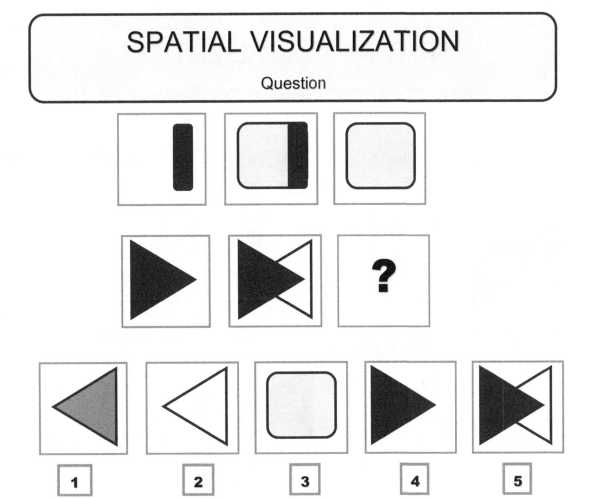

ANSWER: 2

19

SPATIAL VISUALIZATION

SUBTRACT FIGURES (Remove 1st figure from 2nd figure)

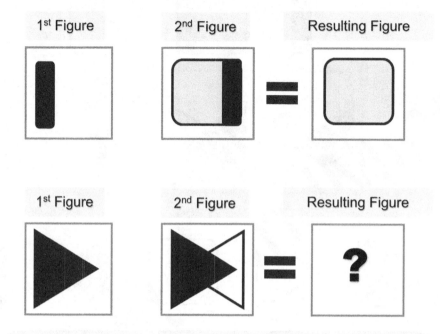

How to solve?

STEP-1: Understand position of figure in 1st Box

Understand position of figure in 2nd Box

STEP-2: Remove 1st Figure from 2nd Figure

NOTE: Pay attention to position of each figure in 3rd figure. Position of each figure **MUST** match with position of figures in 1st and 2nd boxes.

STEP-3: Find the correct Answer

SPATIAL VISUALIZATION

SUBTRACT FIGURES (Remove 1st figure from 2nd figure)

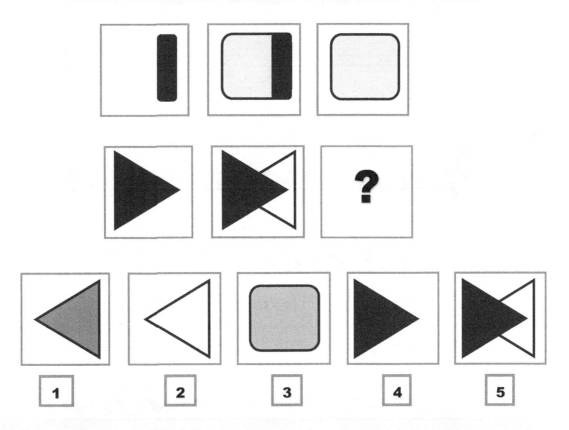

How to solve?

Remove 1st Figure from 2nd Figure

ANSWER: 2

Answer Choice 1 is incorrect. Color is incorrect.

Answer Choice 3 is incorrect. Shape is incorrect.

Answer Choice 4 is incorrect. Other figure is removed.

Answer Choice 5 is incorrect. No figure is removed.

SUBTRACT FIGURES

(Remove 2nd figure from 1st figure)

22

SPATIAL VISUALIZATION

Question

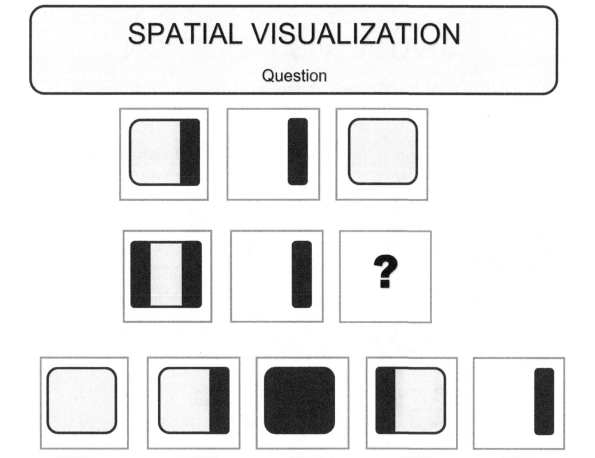

ANSWER: 4

23

SPATIAL VISUALIZATION

SUBTRACT FIGURES (Remove 2nd figure from 1st figure)

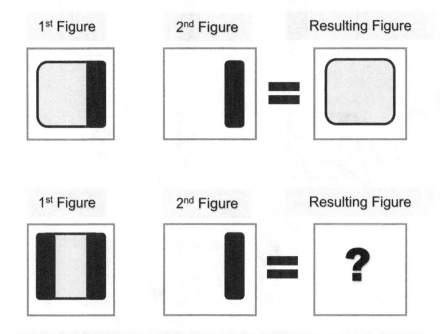

1st Figure	2nd Figure	Resulting Figure

How to solve?

STEP-1: Understand position of figure in 1st Box

Understand position of figure in 2nd Box

STEP-2: Remove 2nd figure from 1st figure

NOTE: Pay attention to position of each figure in 3rd figure. Position of each figure **MUST** match with position of figures in 1st and 2nd boxes.

STEP-3: Find the correct Answer

SPATIAL VISUALIZATION

SUBTRACT FIGURES (Remove 2ⁿᵈ figure from 1ˢᵗ figure)

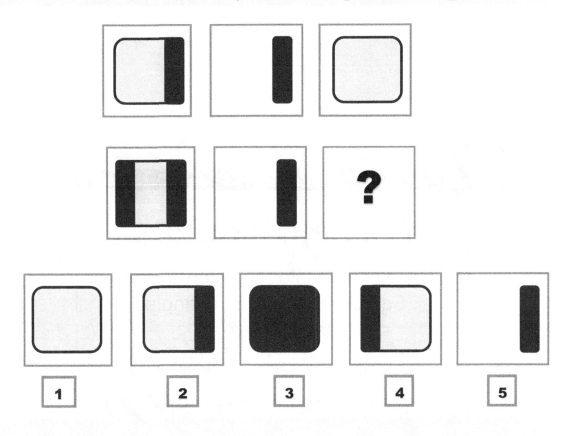

How to solve?

Remove 2ⁿᵈ figure from 1ˢᵗ figure

ANSWER: 4

Answer Choice 1 is incorrect. Both vertical strips are removed.

Answer Choice 2 is incorrect. 2ⁿᵈ figure is not removed.

Answer Choice 3 is incorrect. Color is incorrect.

Answer Choice 5 is incorrect. 2ⁿᵈ figure is shown.

FOLDING FIGURES

(Fold figures into the given space -
Square, Rectangle, Triangle,
Hexagon etc.,)

SPATIAL VISUALIZATION
Folding Figures

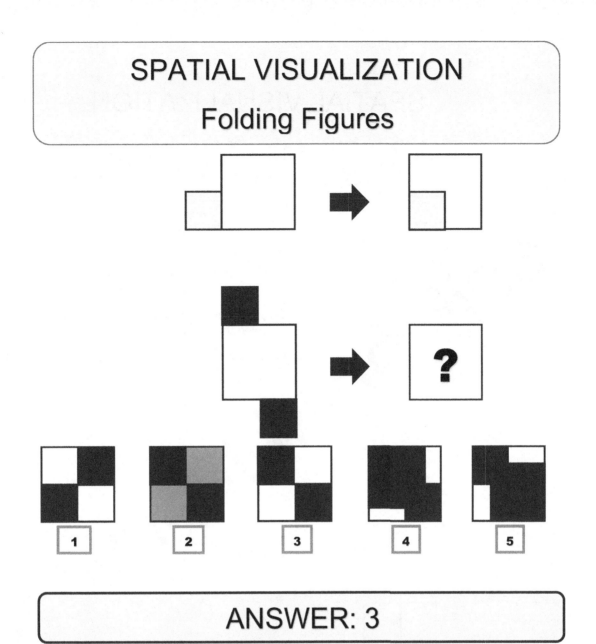

ANSWER: 3

Step#1: Identify all figures that are outside the space.

In this question there are 2 squares outside the space.

Step#2: Identify all points where figures are touching the SPACE.

In this question there are 4 points (marked as ●)

Step#3: Use **Reflection (FLIP)** to fold each figure into the inside space.

SPATIAL VISUALIZATION
Folding Figures – How to solve?

Figure

Reflection (Flip)
Technique

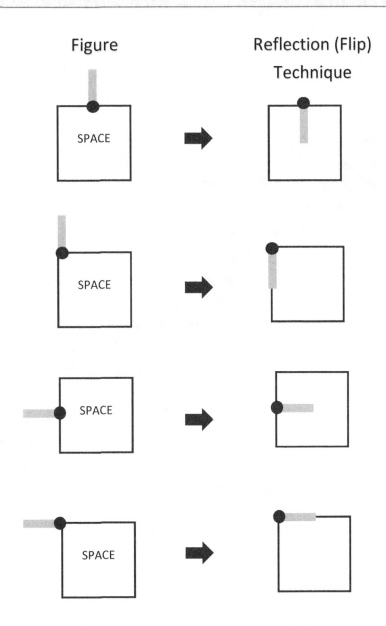

SPATIAL VISUALIZATION
Folding Figures – How to solve?

Figure

Reflection (Flip)
Technique

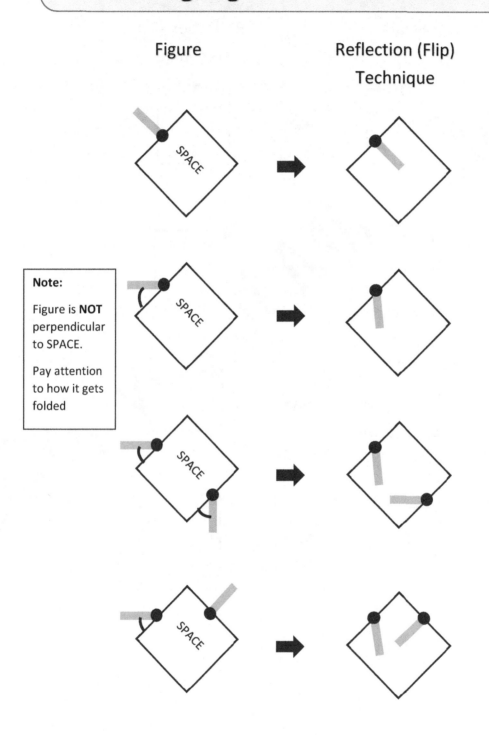

Note:

Figure is **NOT** perpendicular to SPACE.

Pay attention to how it gets folded

SPATIAL VISUALIZATION
Folding Figures – How to solve?

Figure   Reflection (Flip)
Technique

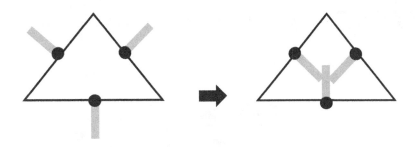

Note:

Figures are **NOT** perpendicular to SPACE.

Pay attention to how it gets folded

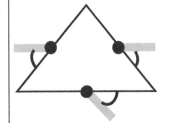 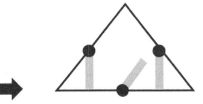

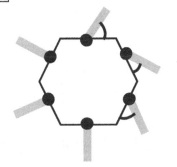 

SPATIAL VISUALIZATION
Folding Figures – How to solve?

Figure

Reflection (Flip)

Technique

Note:

Figures are **NOT** perpendicular to SPACE.

Pay attention to how it gets folded

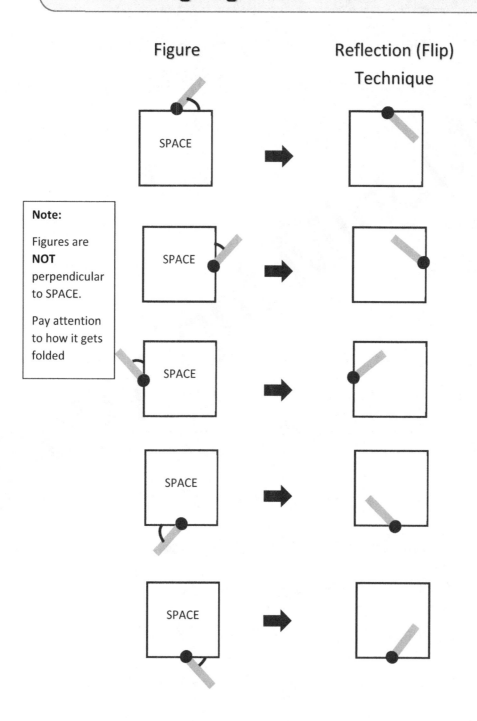

SPATIAL VISUALIZATION
Folding Figures – How to solve?

Figure

Reflection (Flip)
Technique

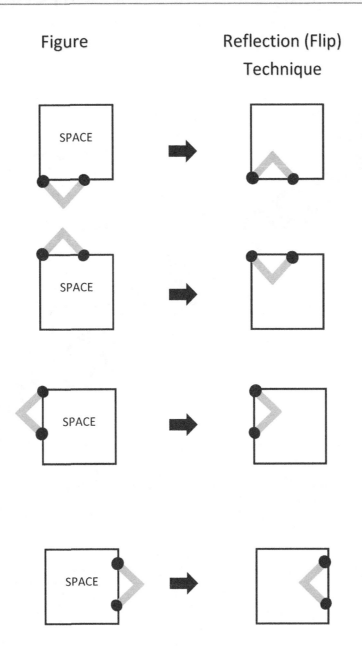

SPATIAL VISUALIZATION
Folding Figures – How to solve?

Figure   Reflection (Flip)
                Technique

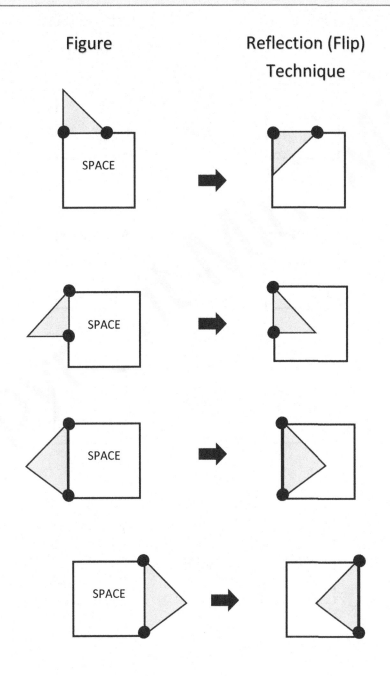

SPATIAL VISUALIZATION
Folding Figures – How to solve?

Figure   Reflection (Flip)
Technique

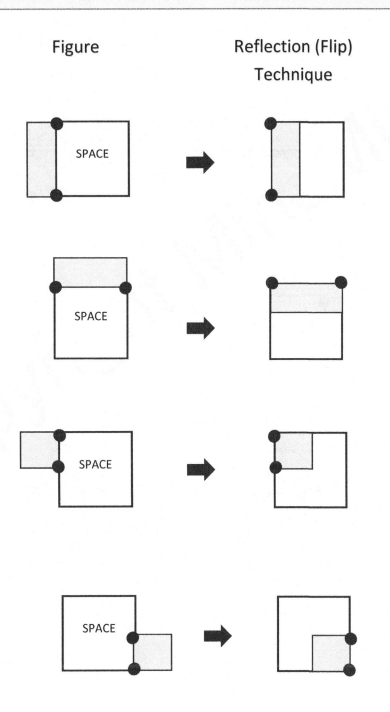

SPATIAL VISUALIZATION
Folding Figures – How to solve?

Figure

Reflection (Flip)
Technique

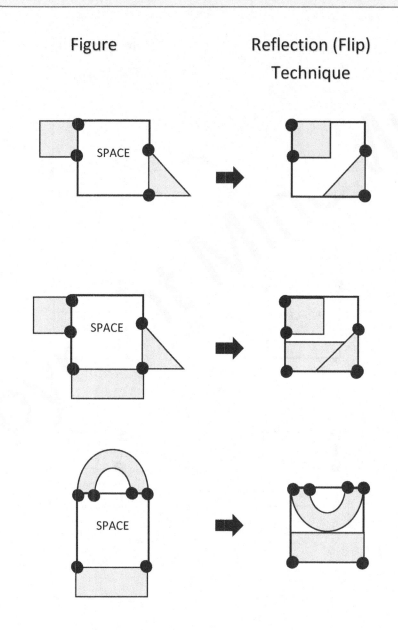

SPATIAL VISUALIZATION
Folding Figures

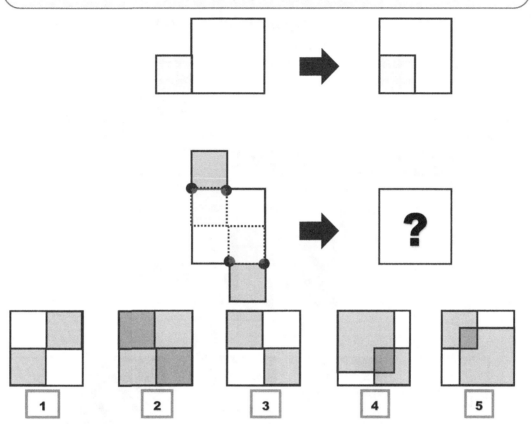

1   2   3   4   5

ANSWER: 3

Answer choices 1,2,4,5 are incorrect.

SPATIAL VISUALIZATION
Folding Figures

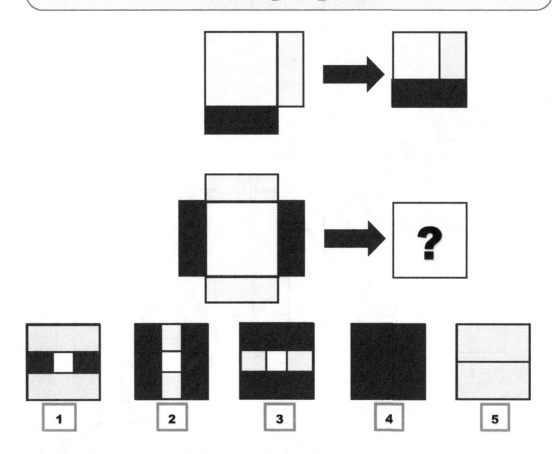

ANSWER: 2

Answer choices 1,3,4,5 are incorrect. In the example,
Black figures are folded on top of Gray figures. So,
answer choice 1 is incorrect.

SPATIAL VISUALIZATION
Folding Figures

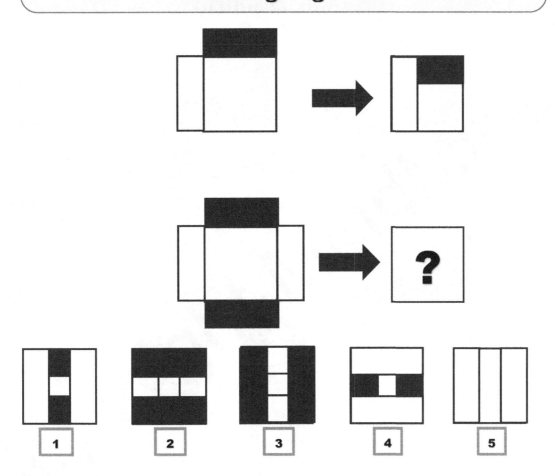

ANSWER: 1

Answer choices 2,3,4,5 are incorrect. In the example,
White figures are folded on top of Black figures. So,
answer choice 2 is incorrect.

S
P
A
T
I
A
L

V
I
S
U
A
L
I
Z
A
T
I
O
N

A
D
D

F
I
G
U
R
E
S

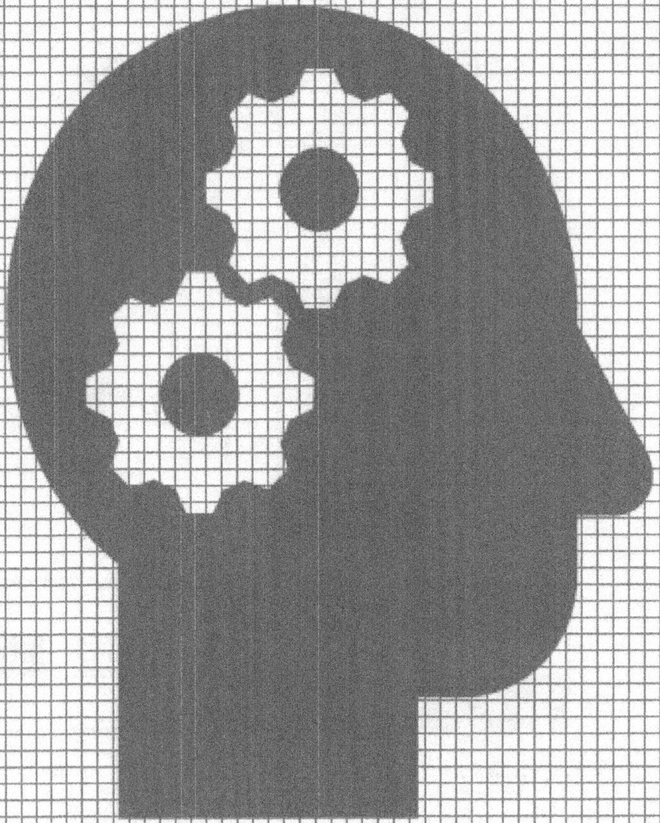

GIFTED & TALENTED

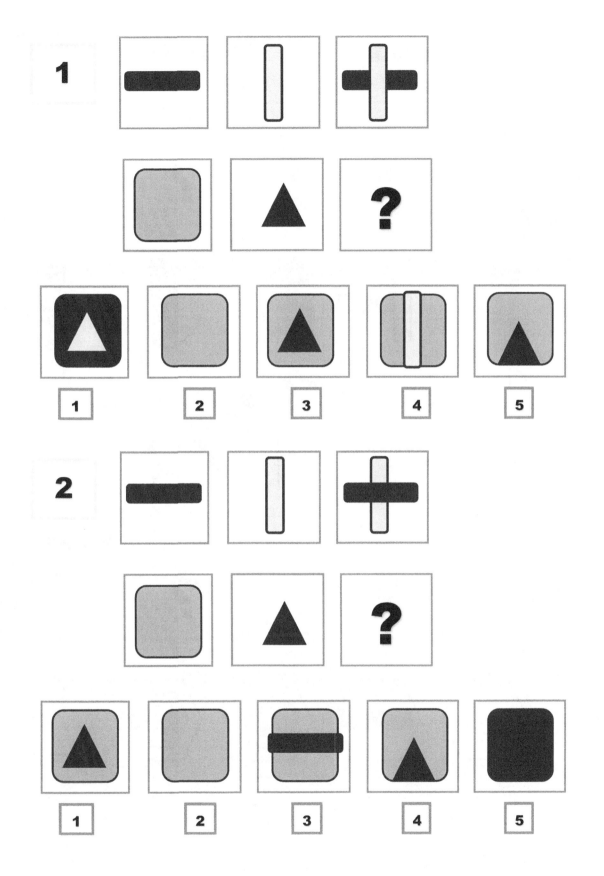

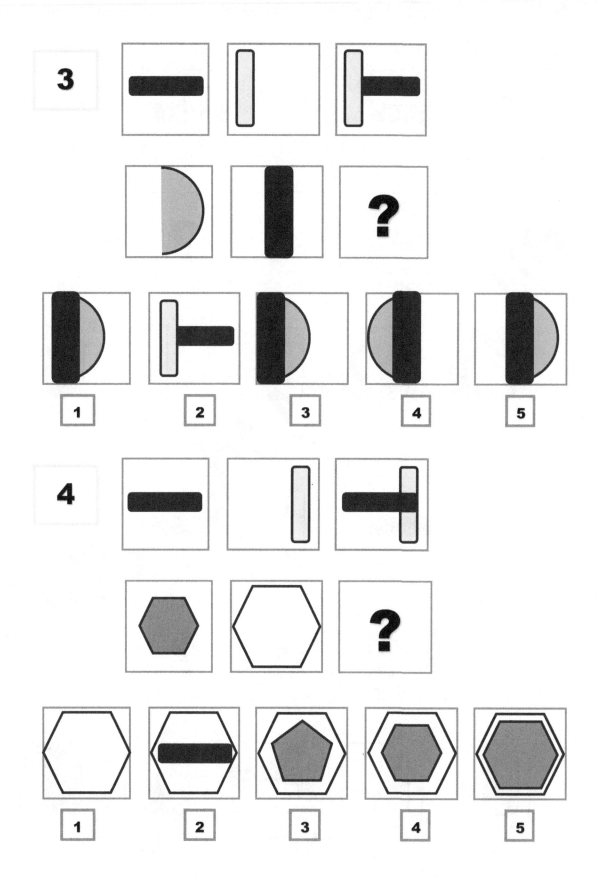

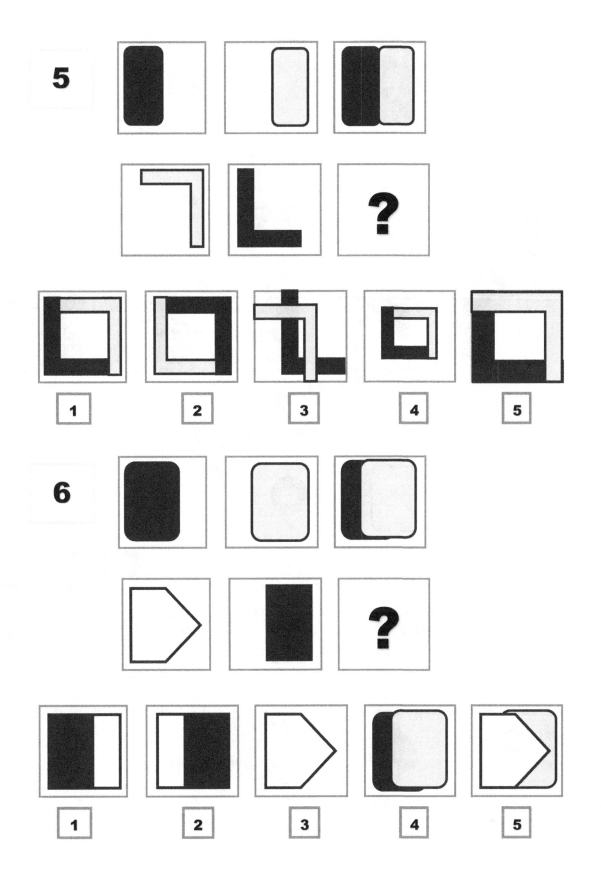

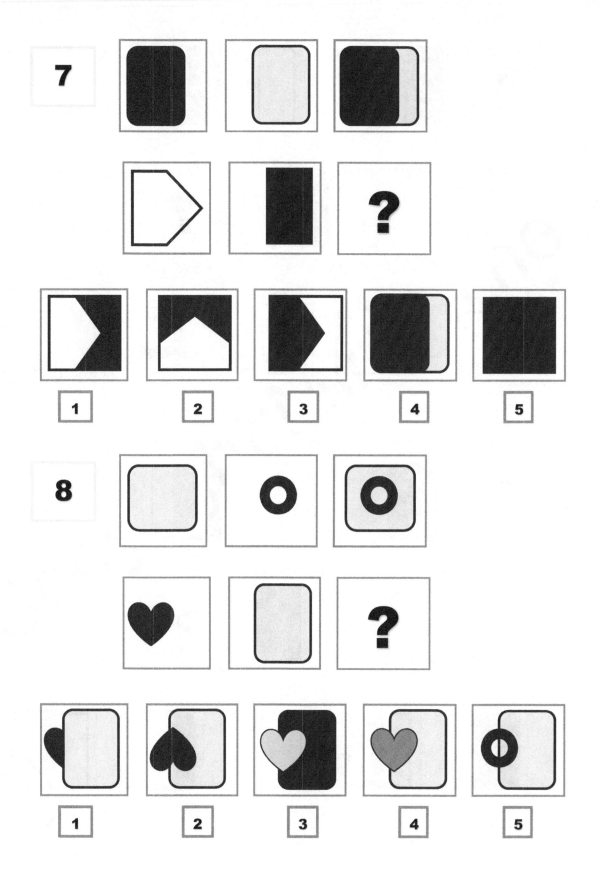

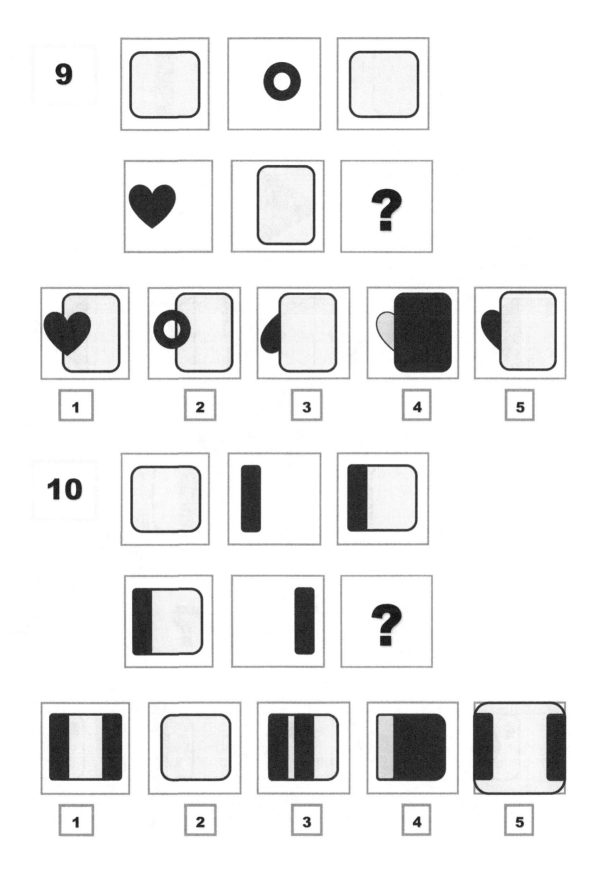

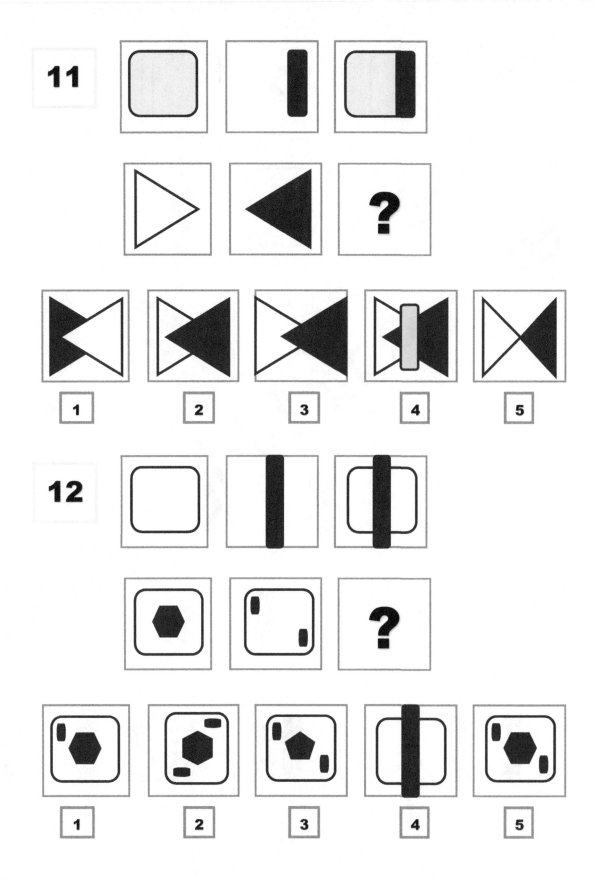

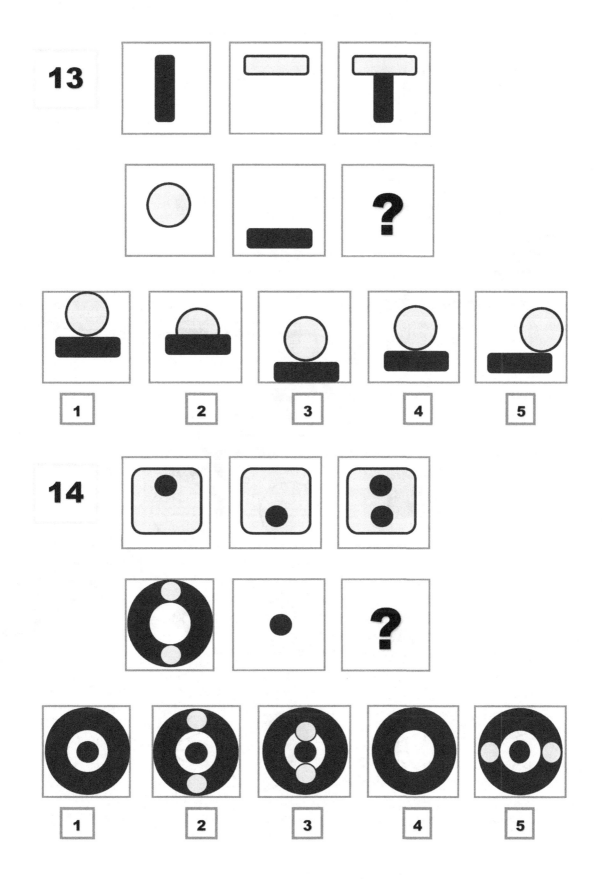

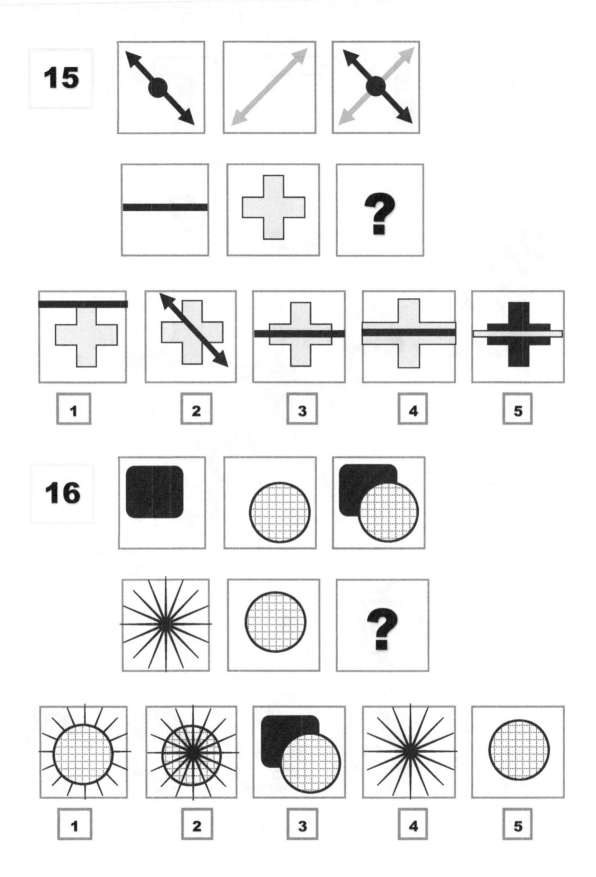

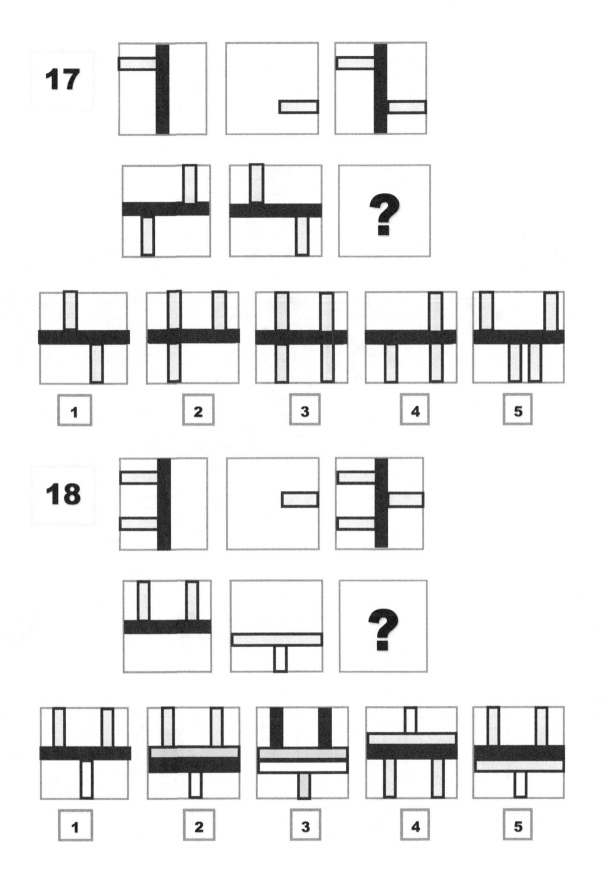

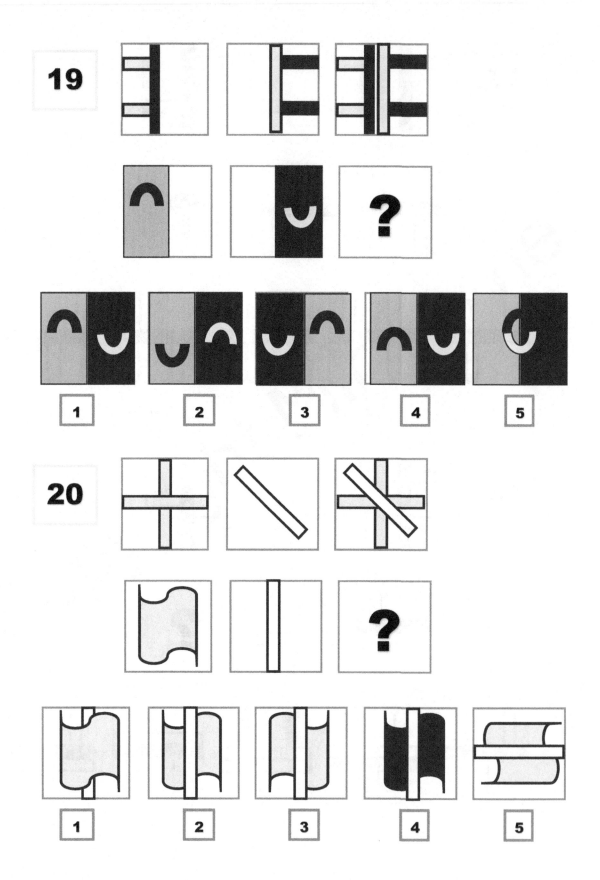

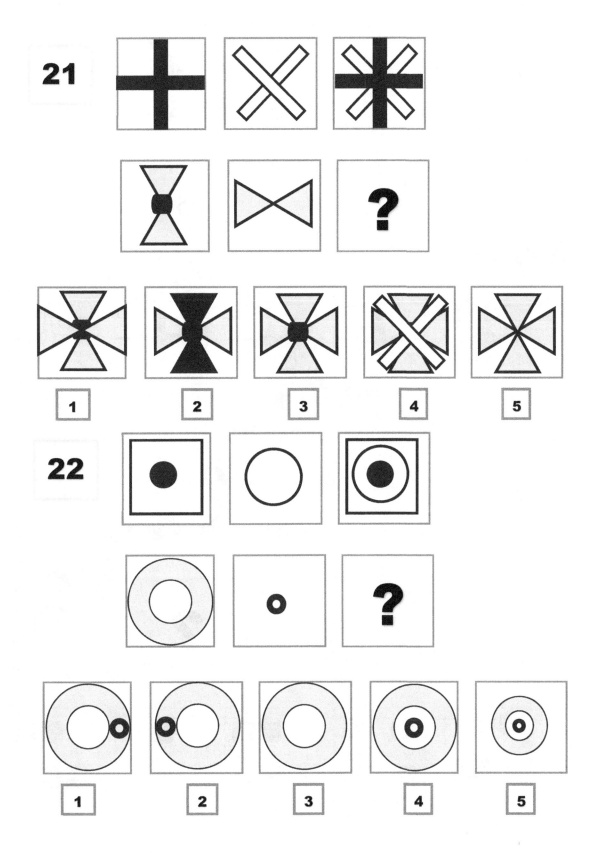

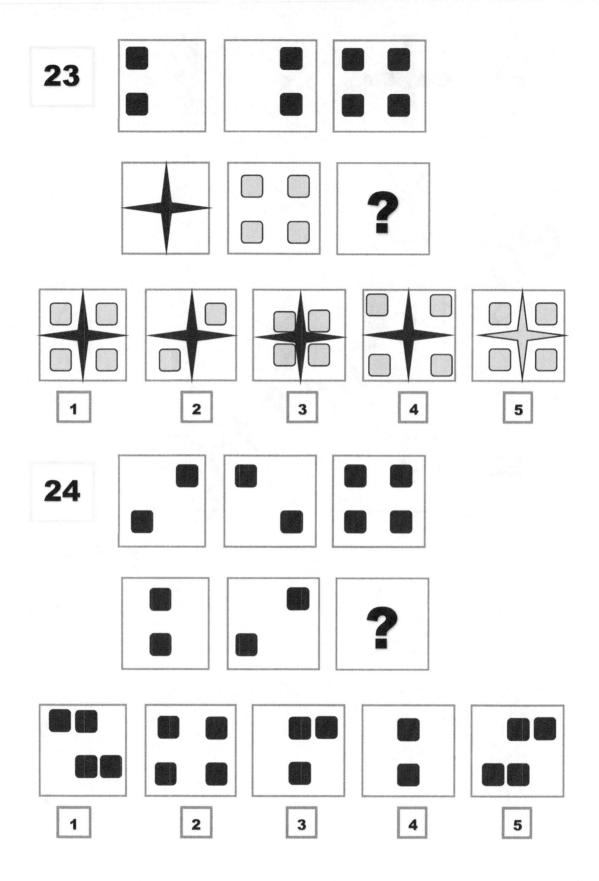

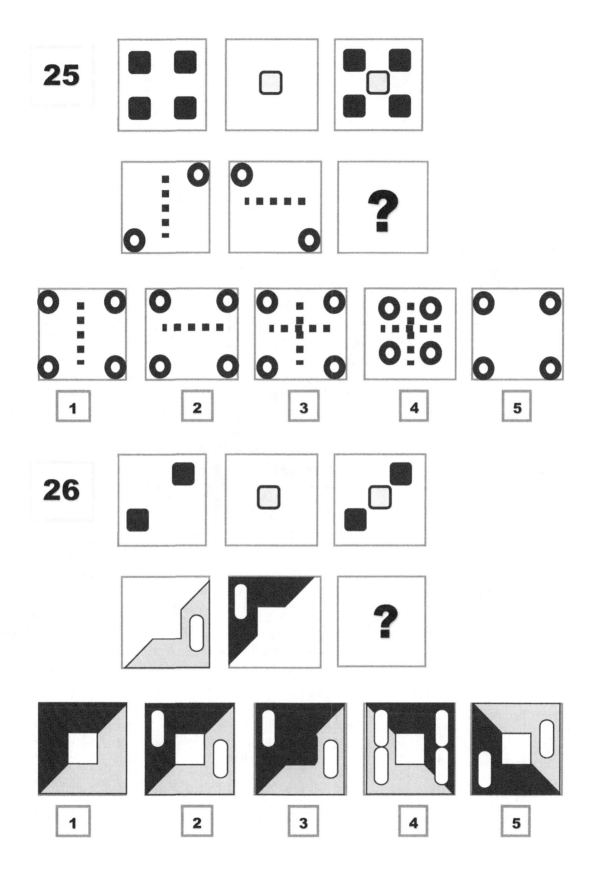

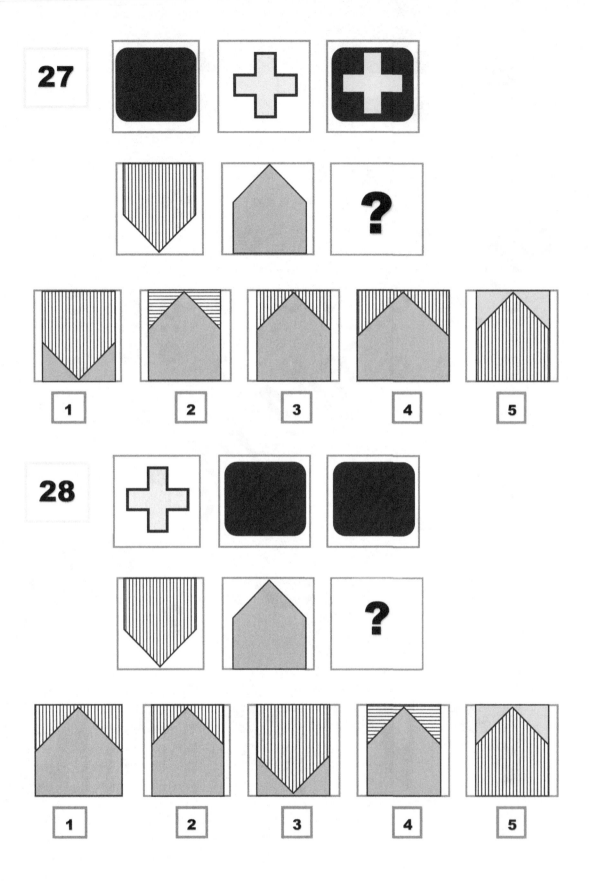

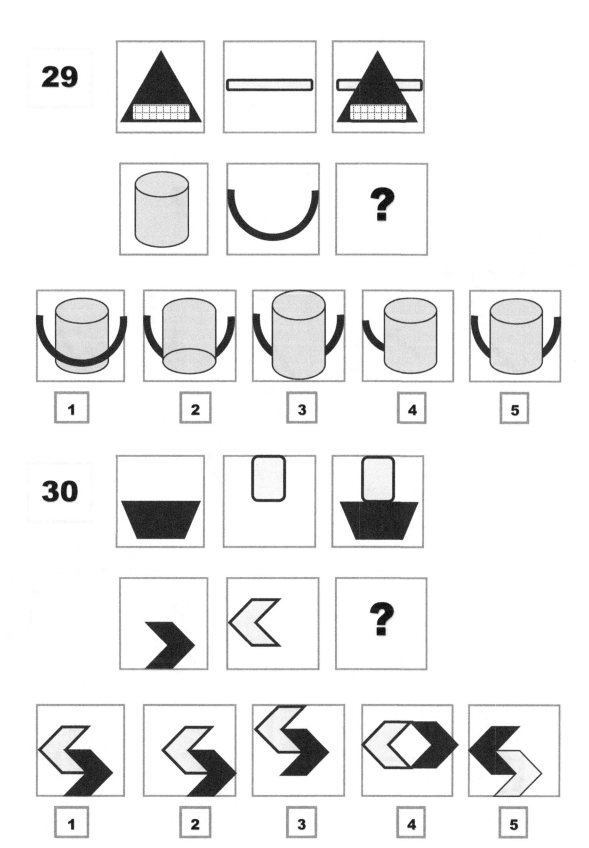

55

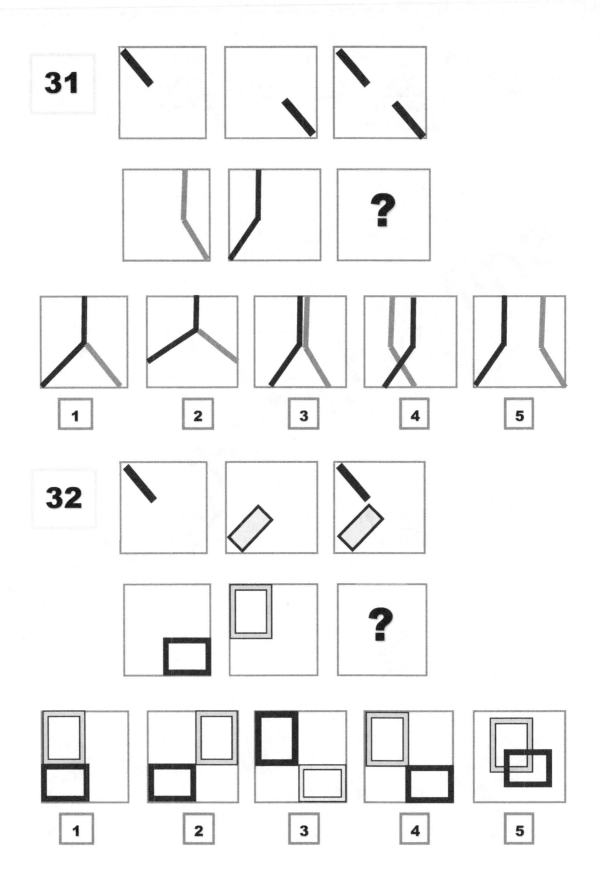

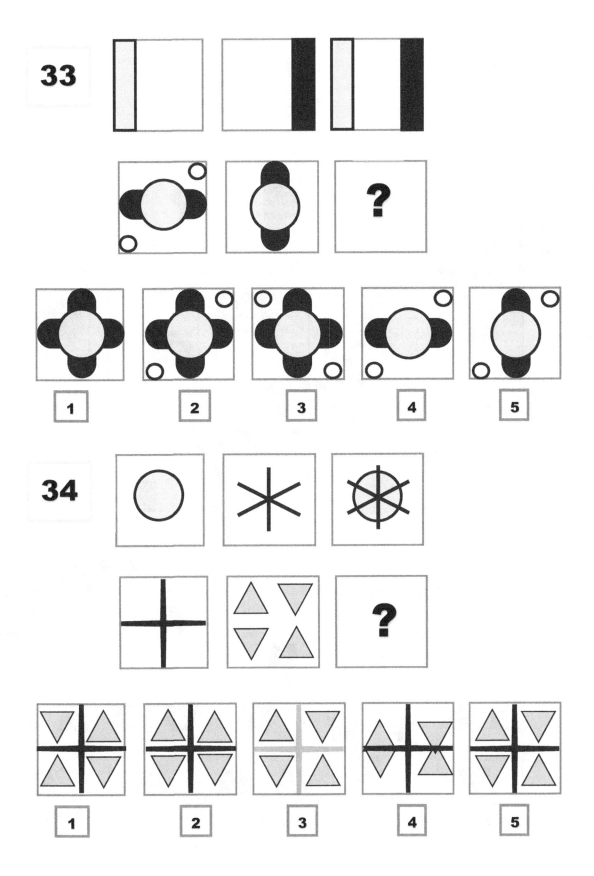

35

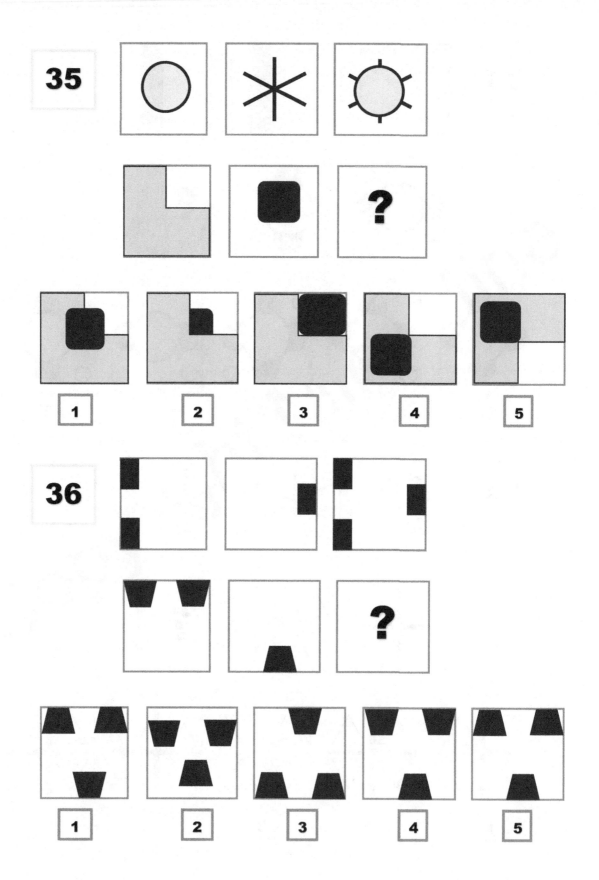

36

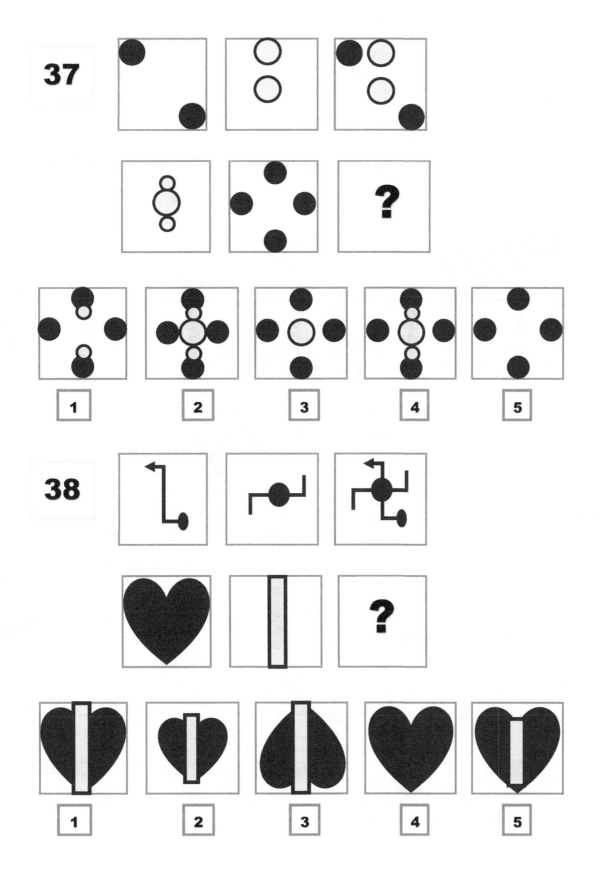

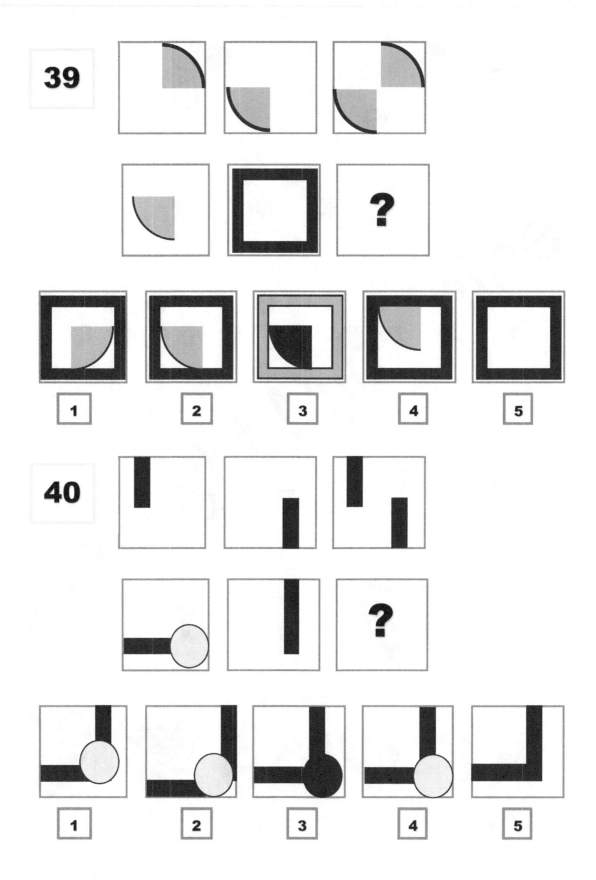

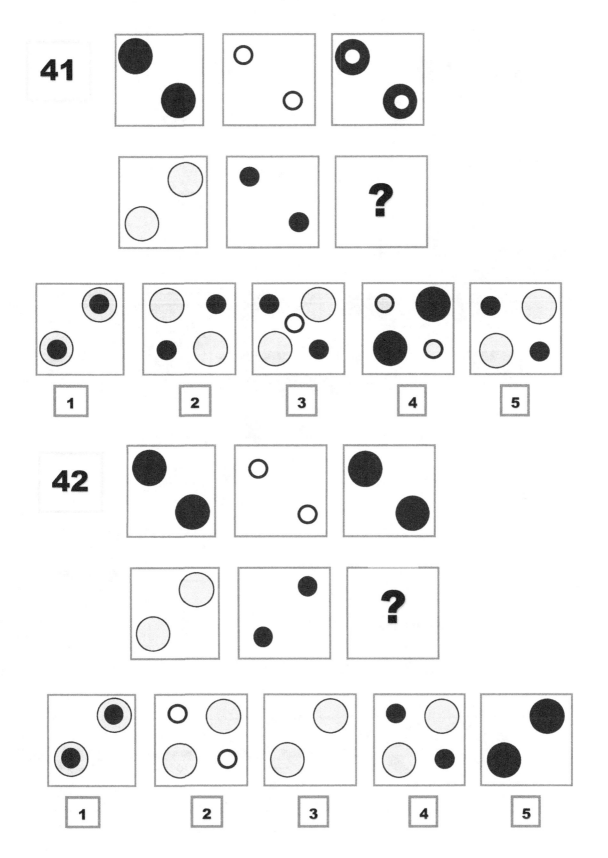

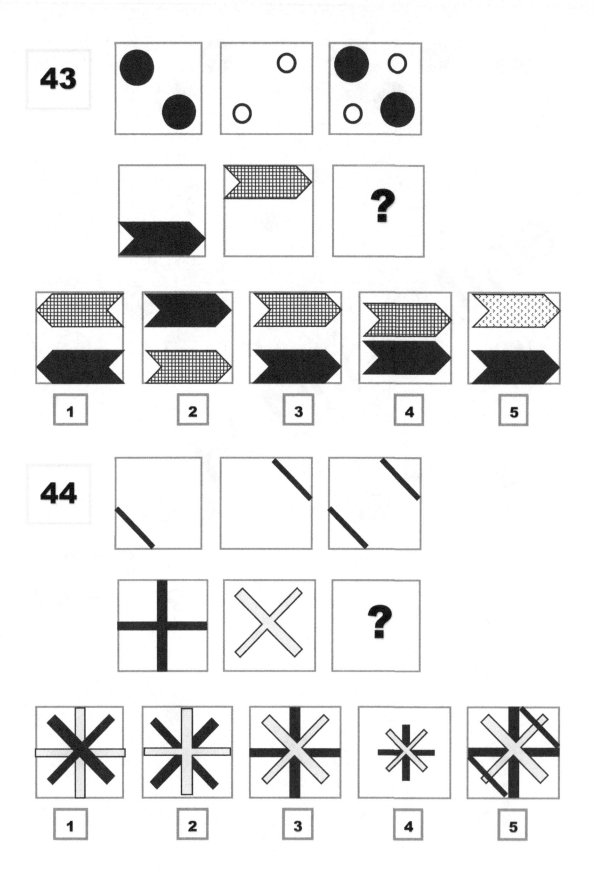

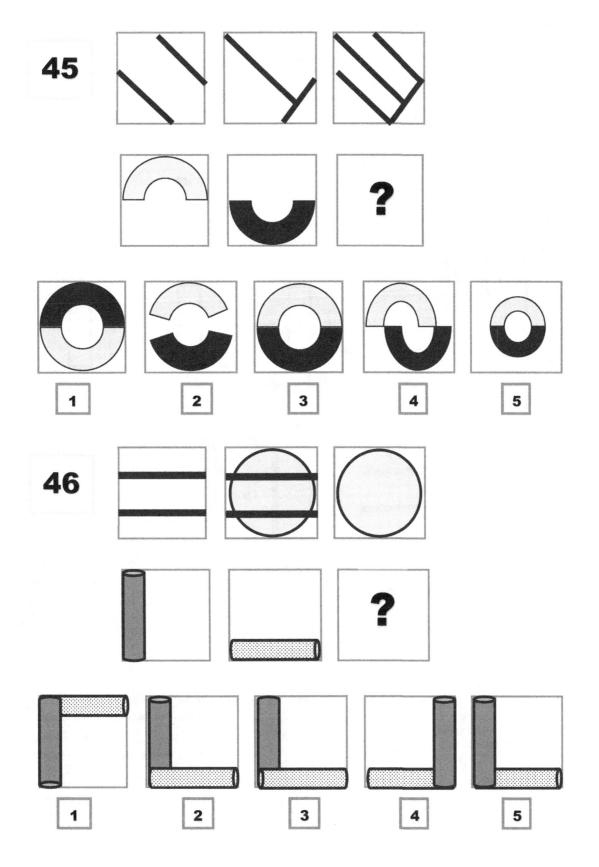

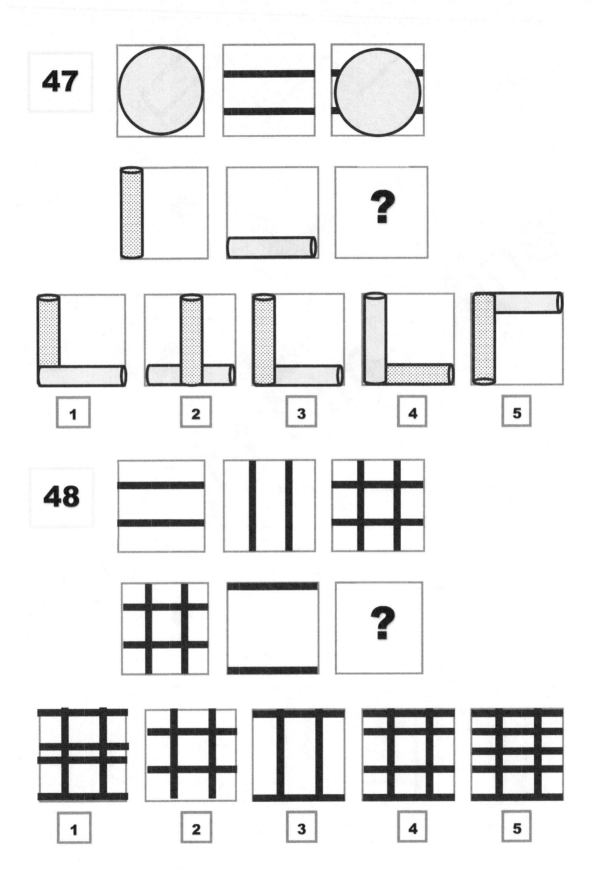

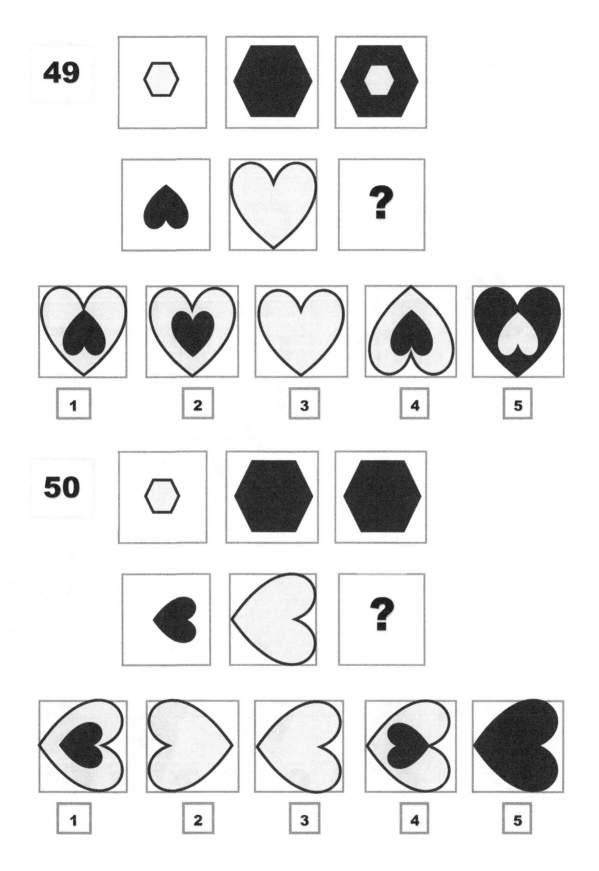

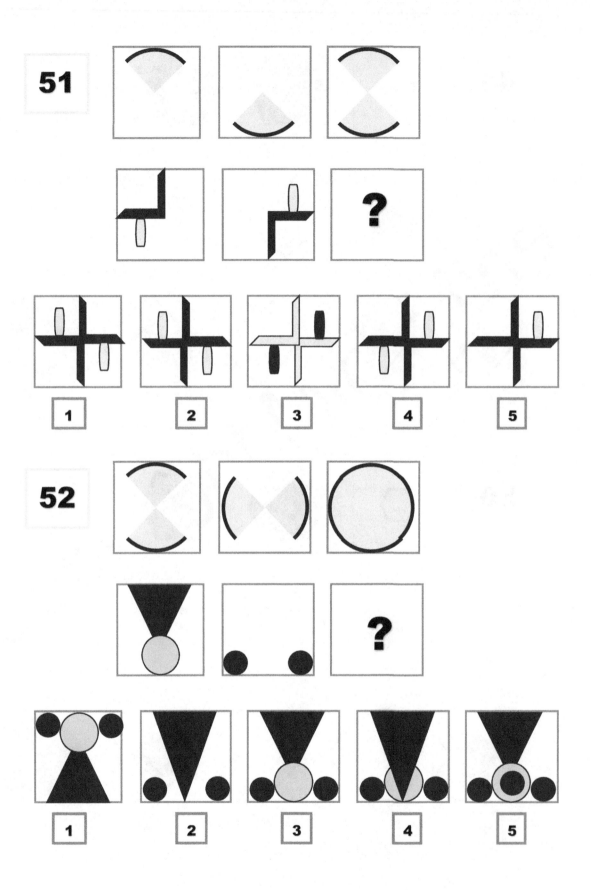

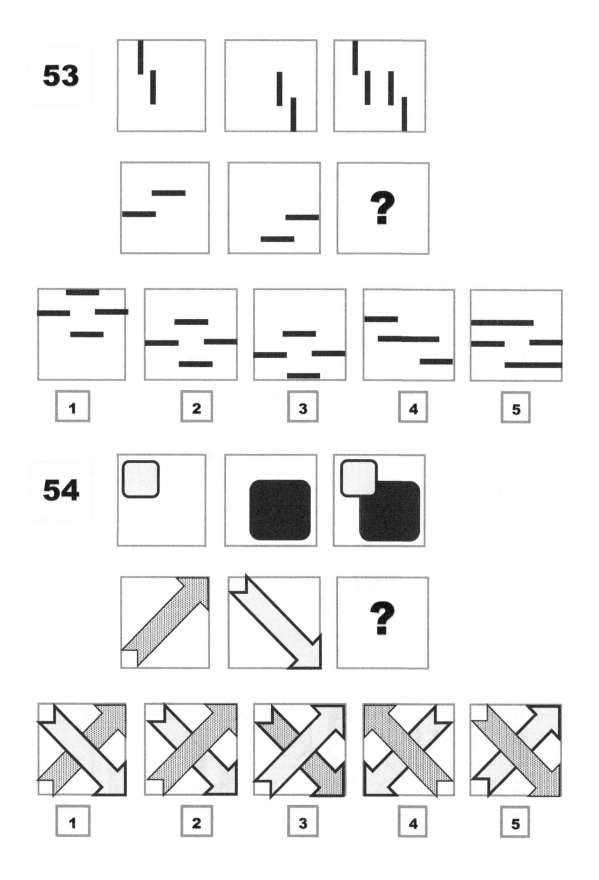

53

54

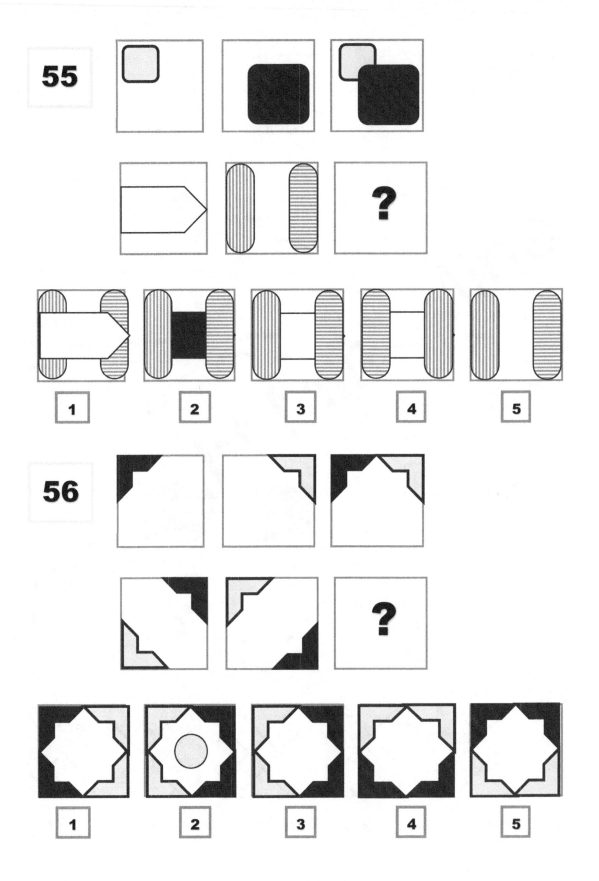

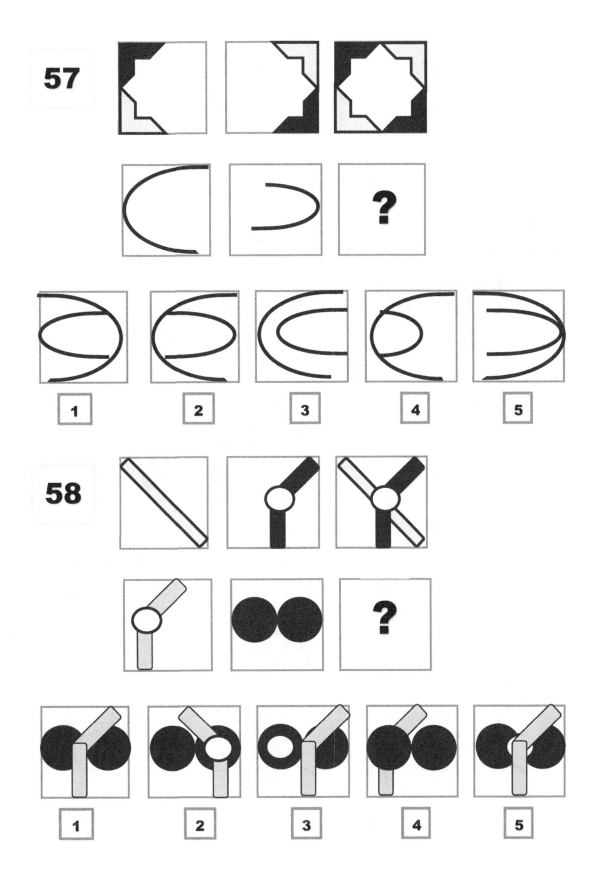

57

58

69

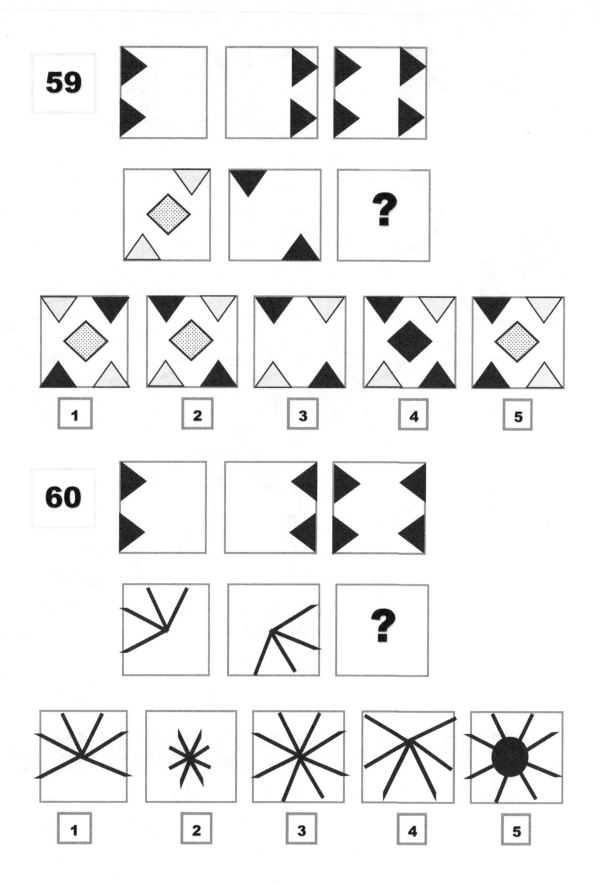

61

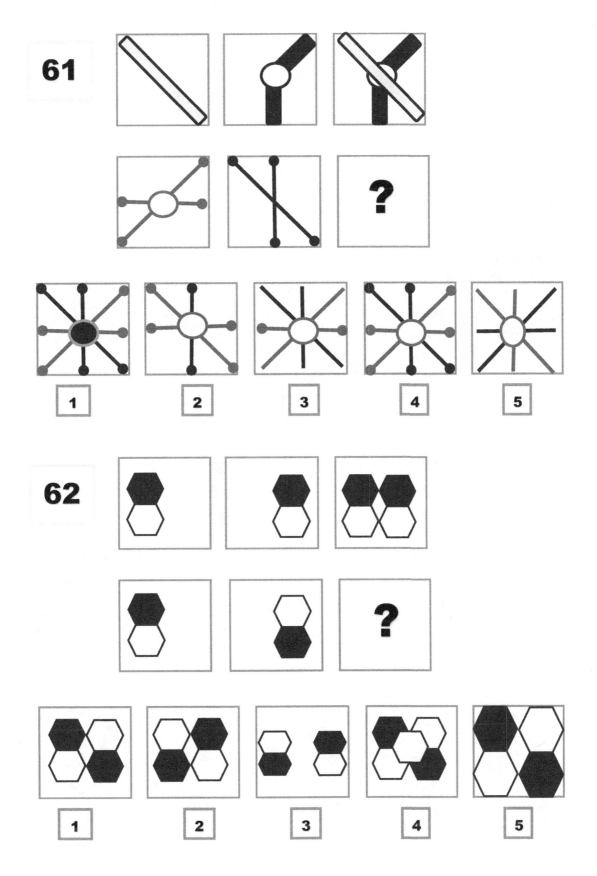

62

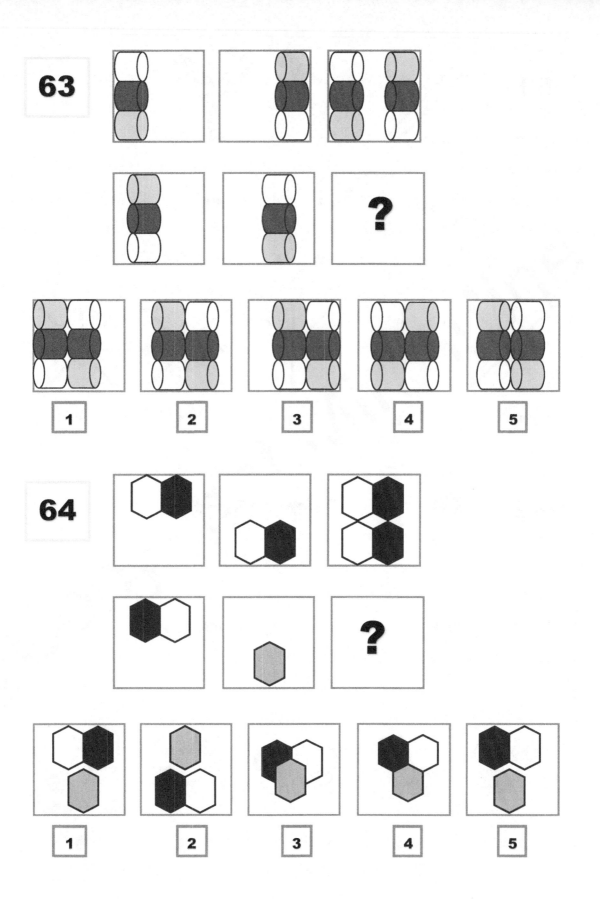

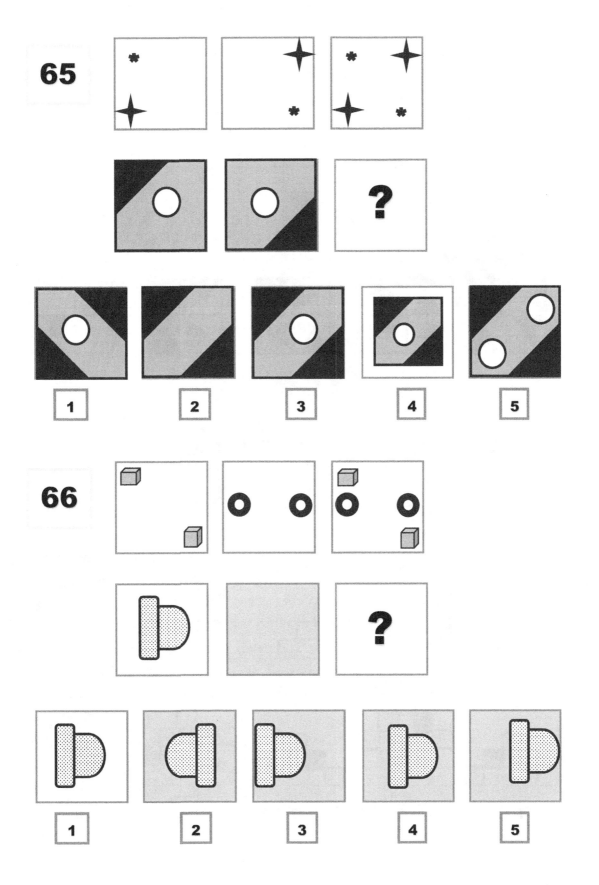

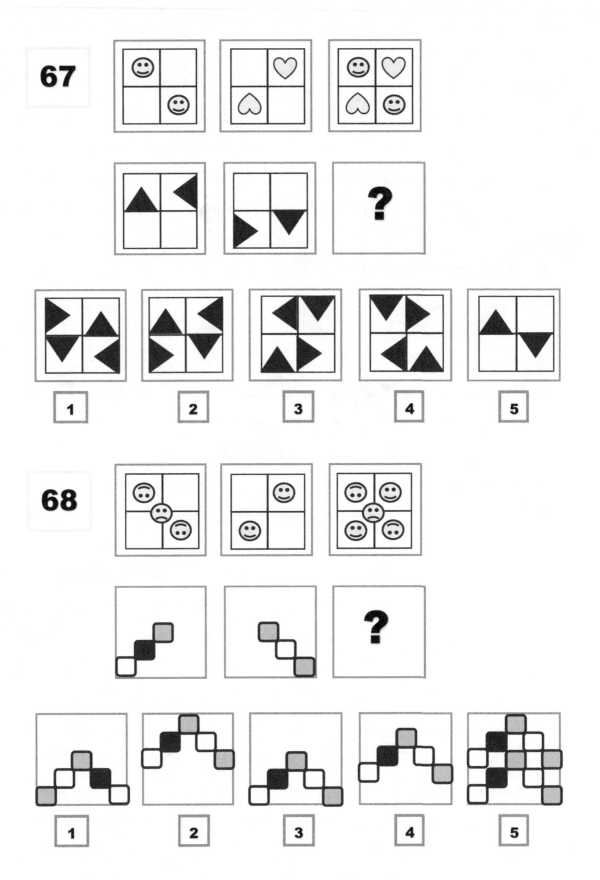

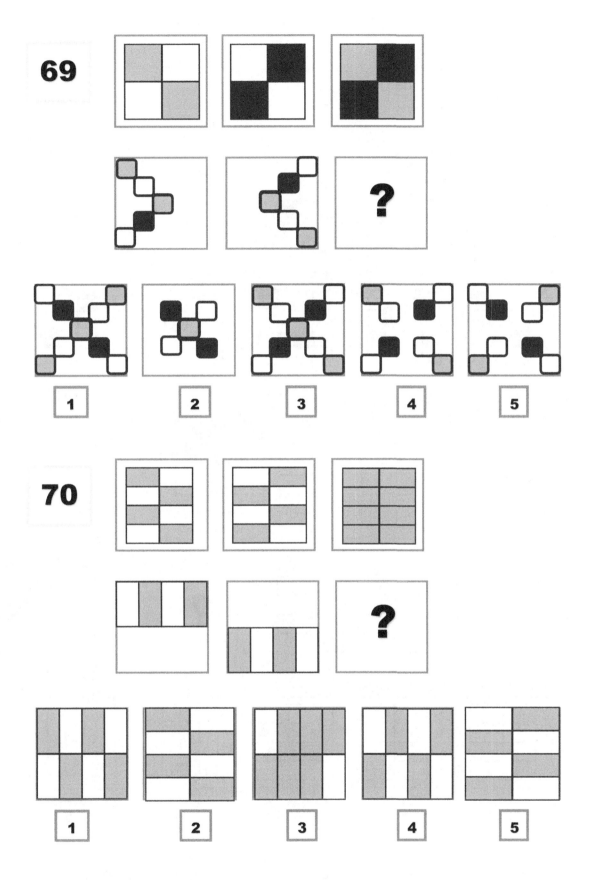

71

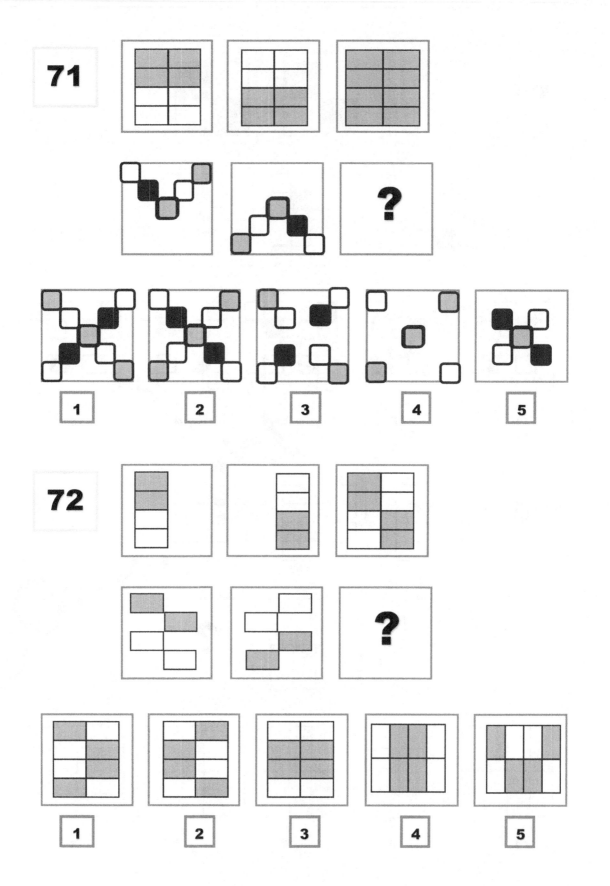

72

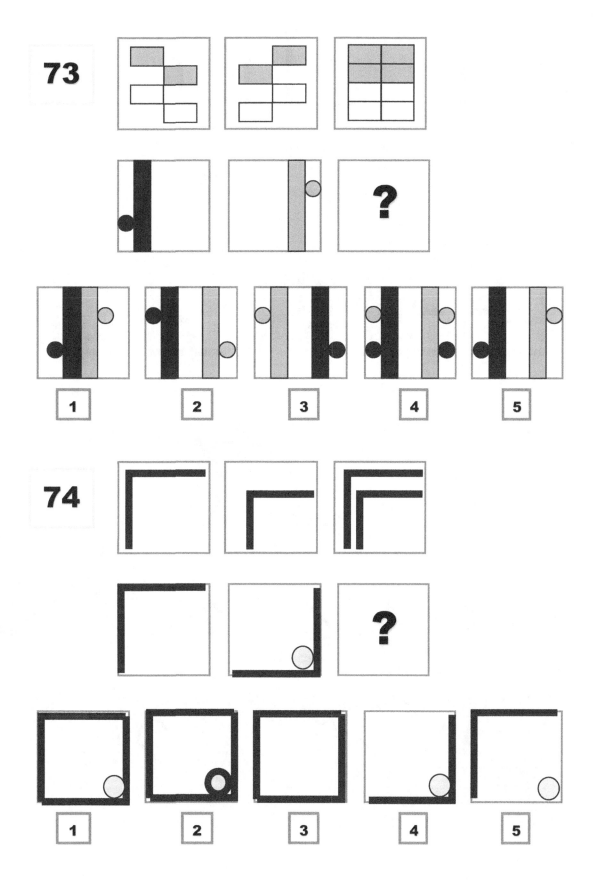

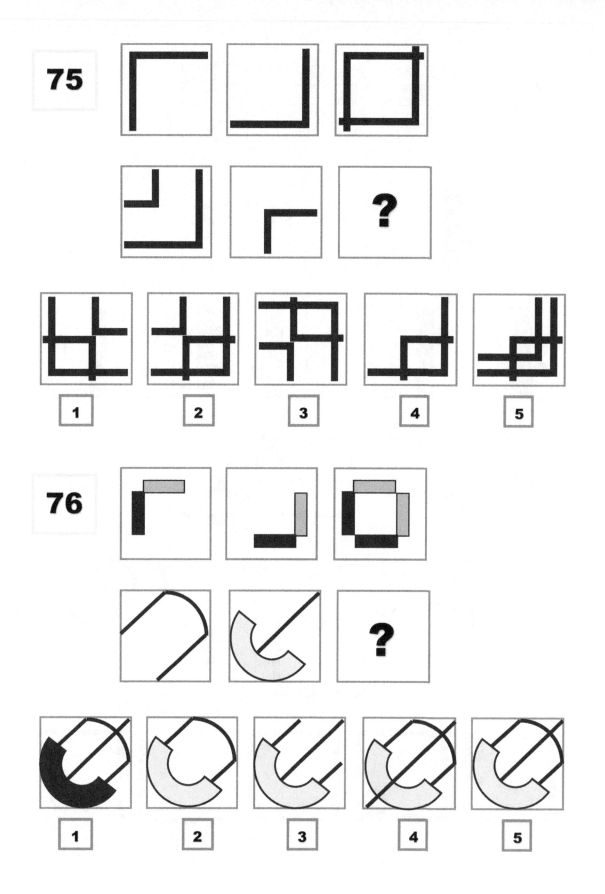

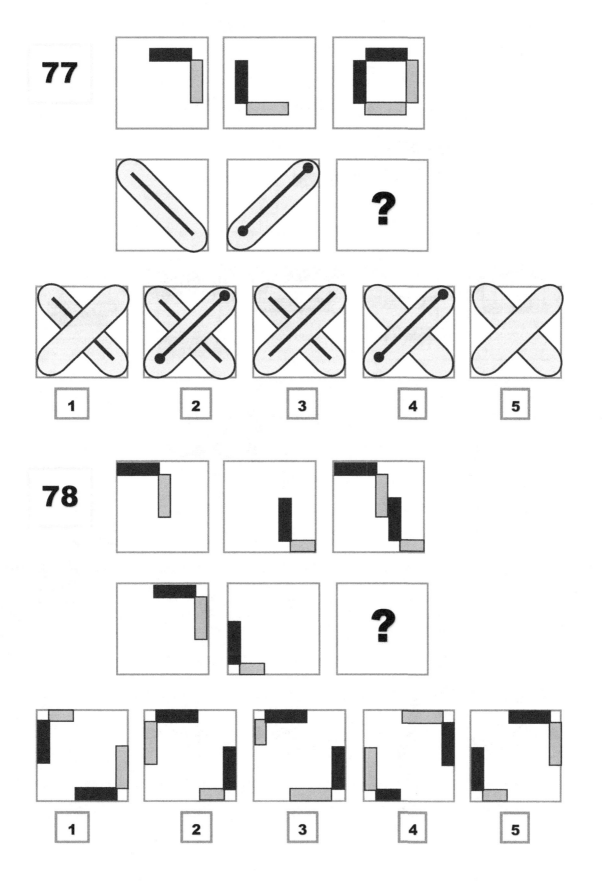

79

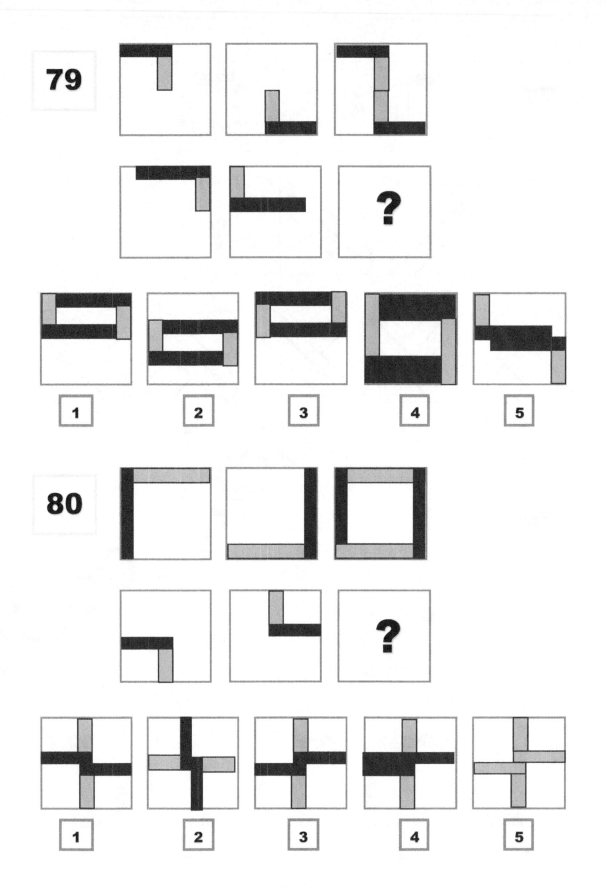

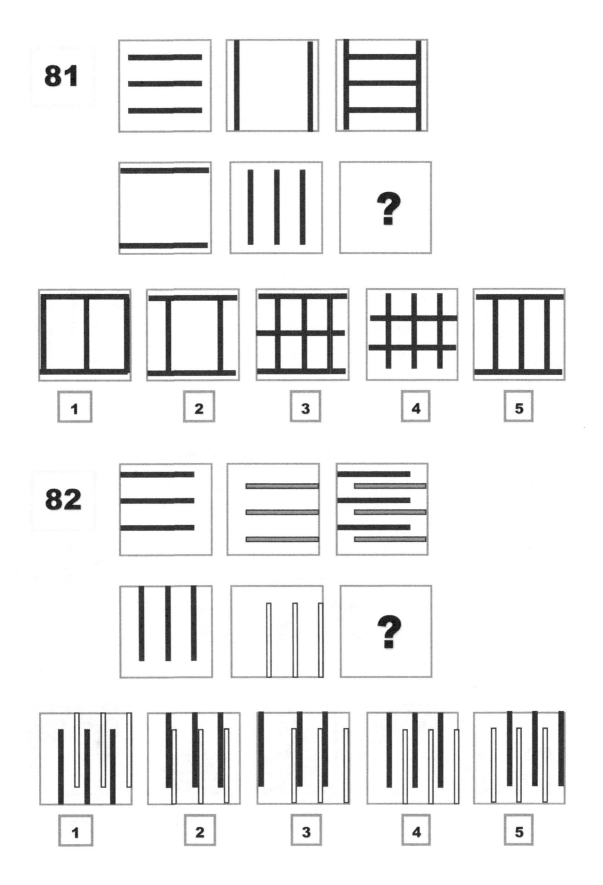

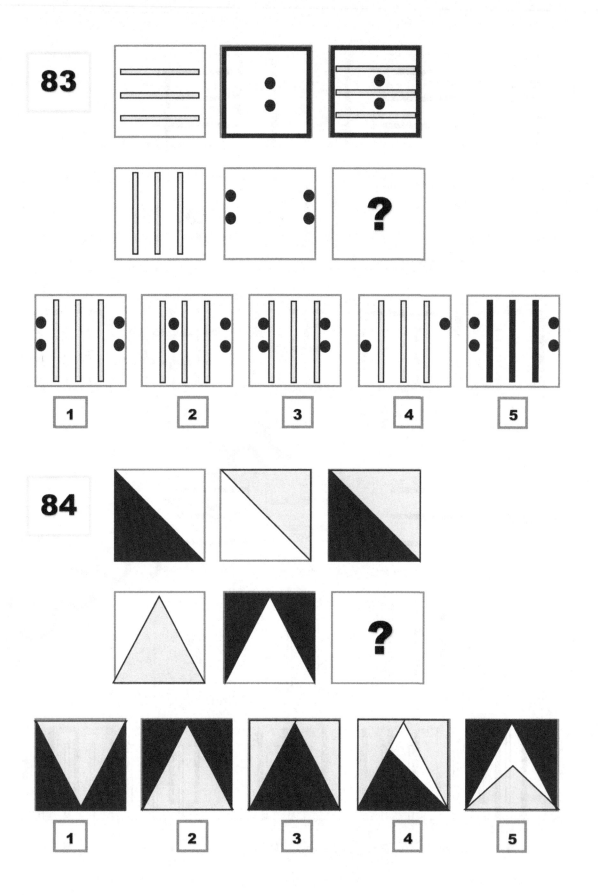

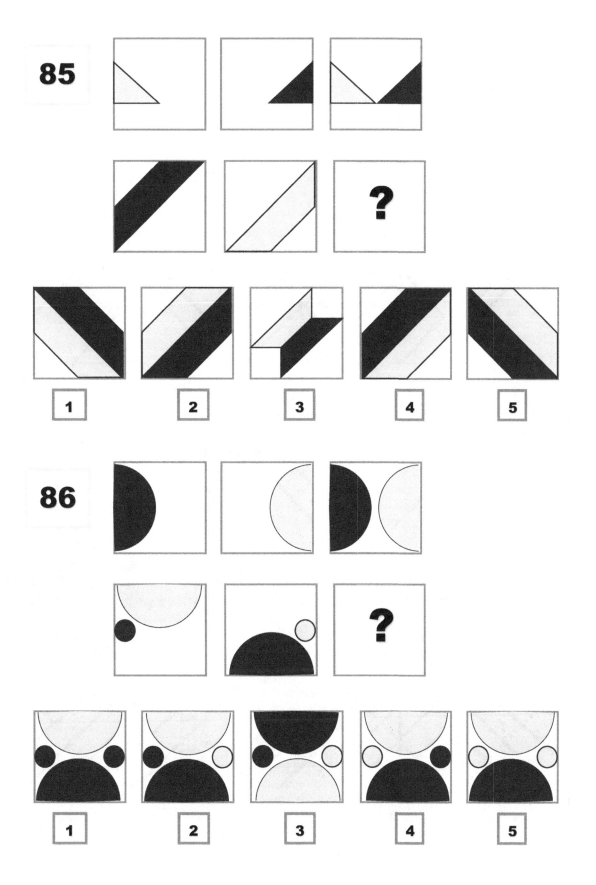

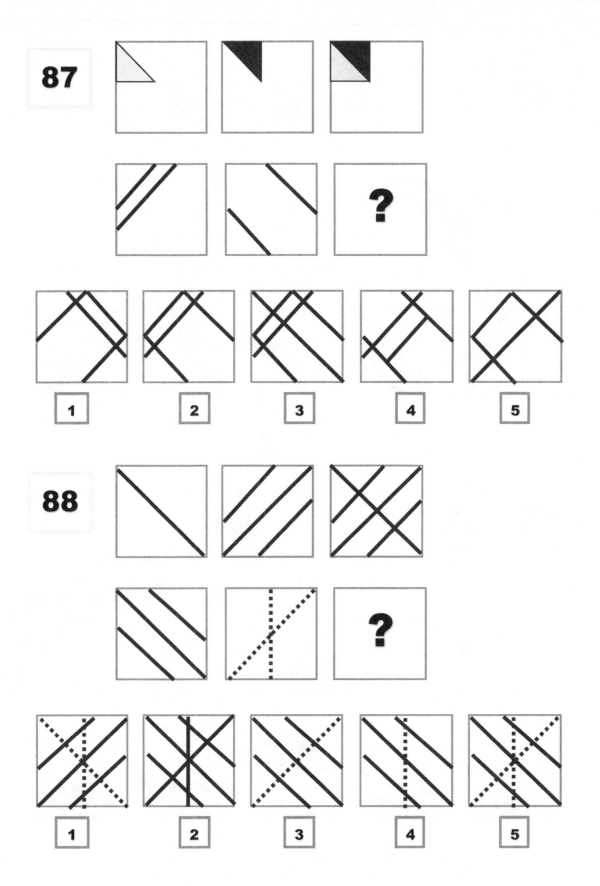

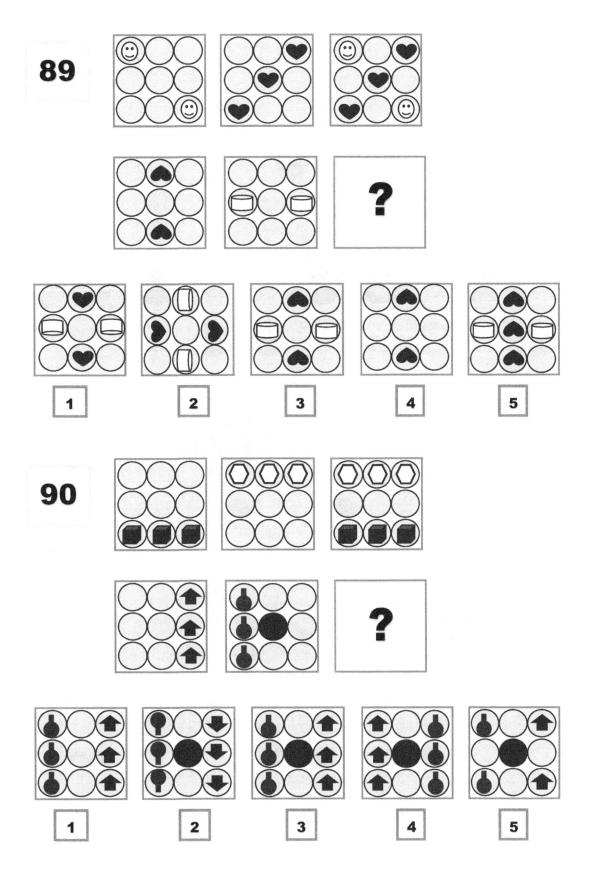

91

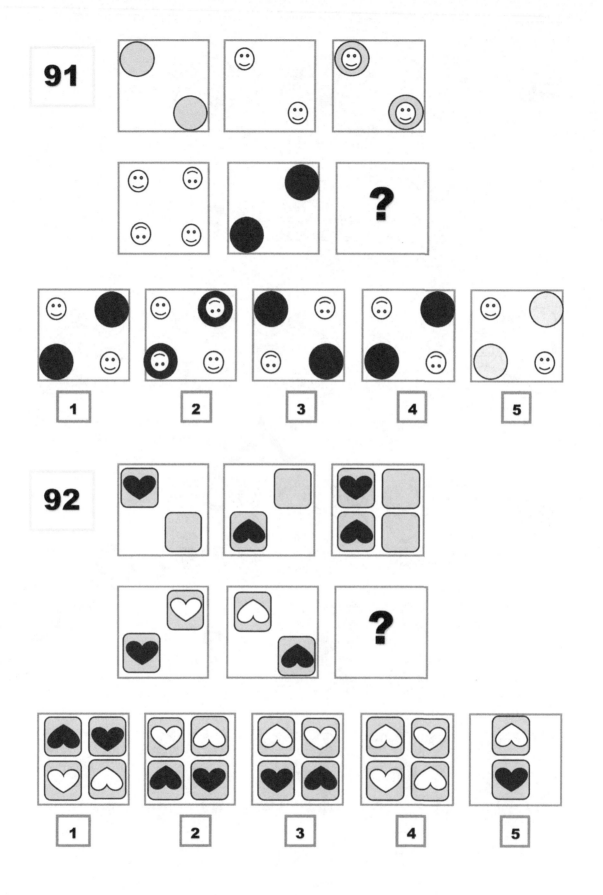

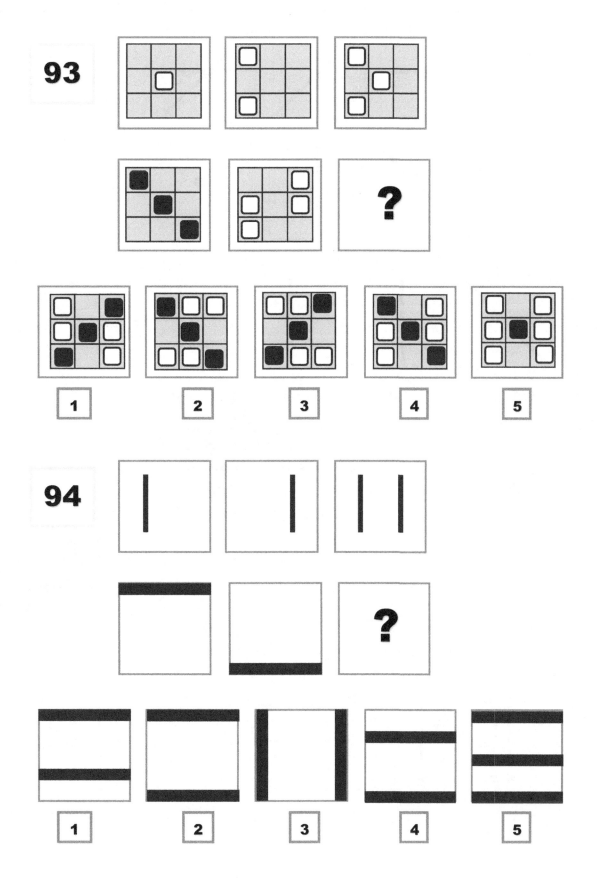

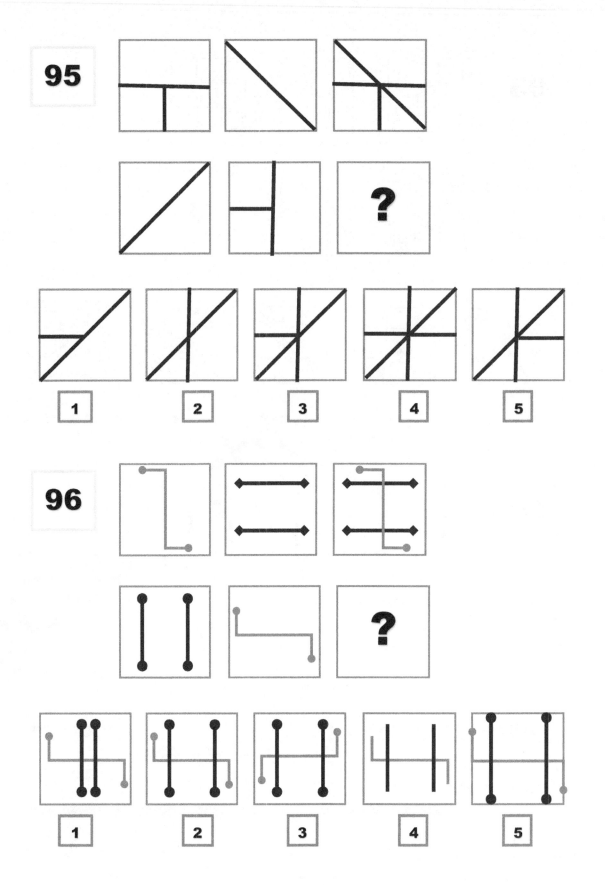

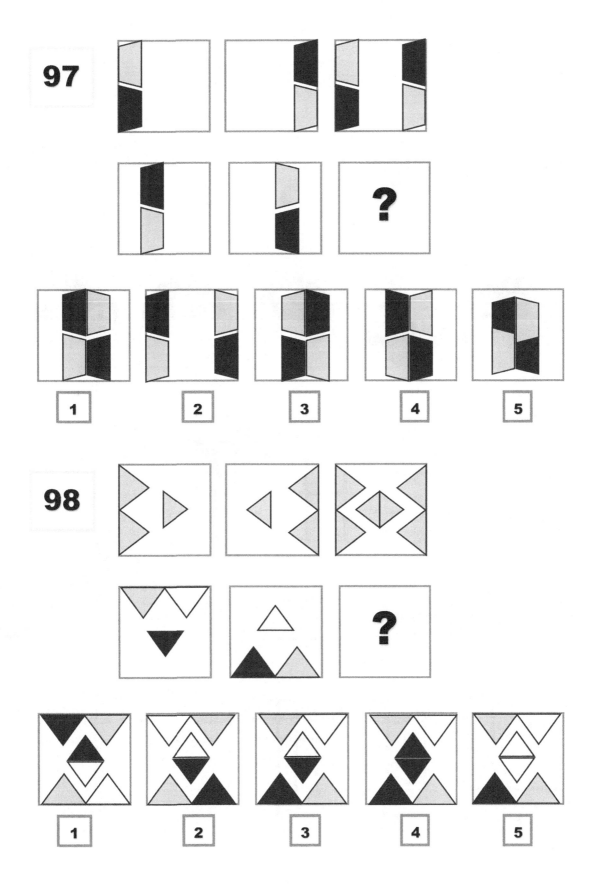

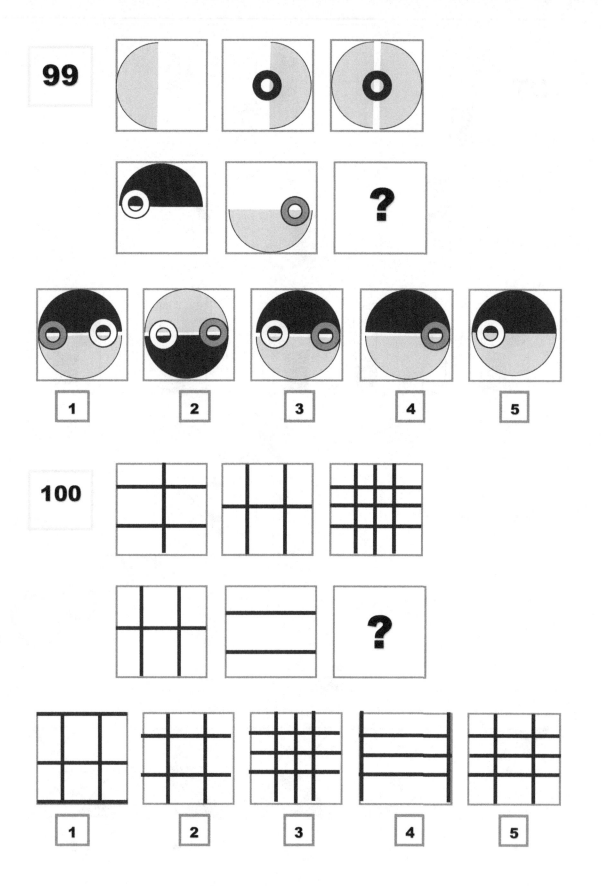

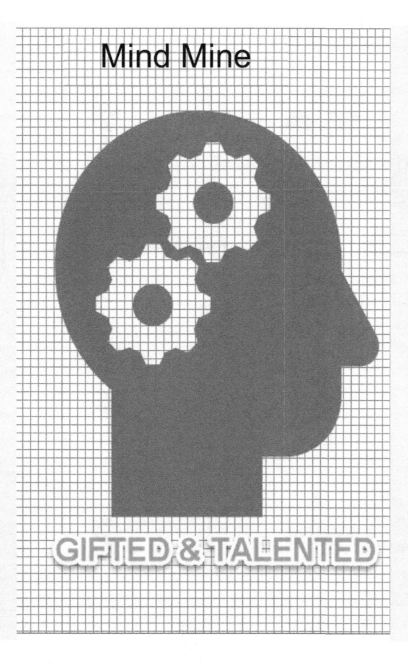

GIFTED & TALENTED

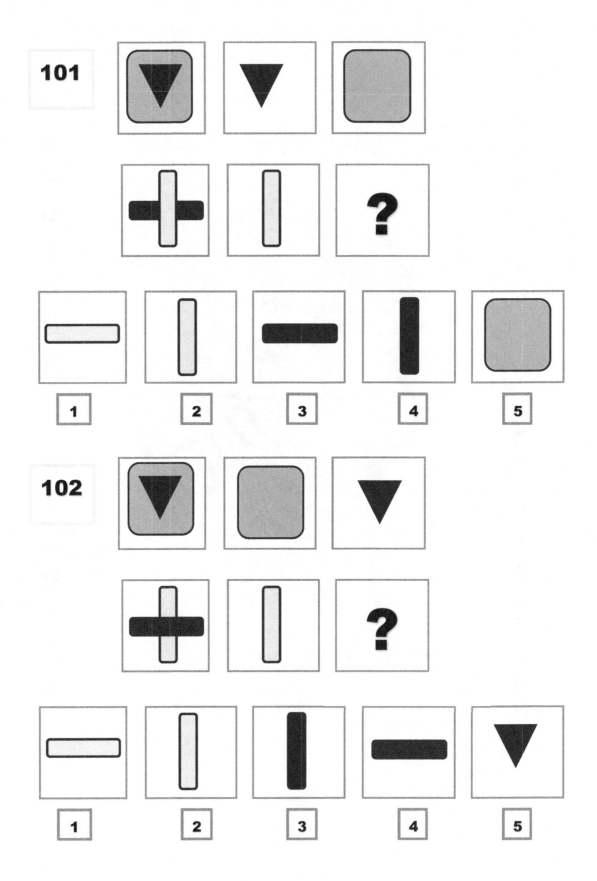

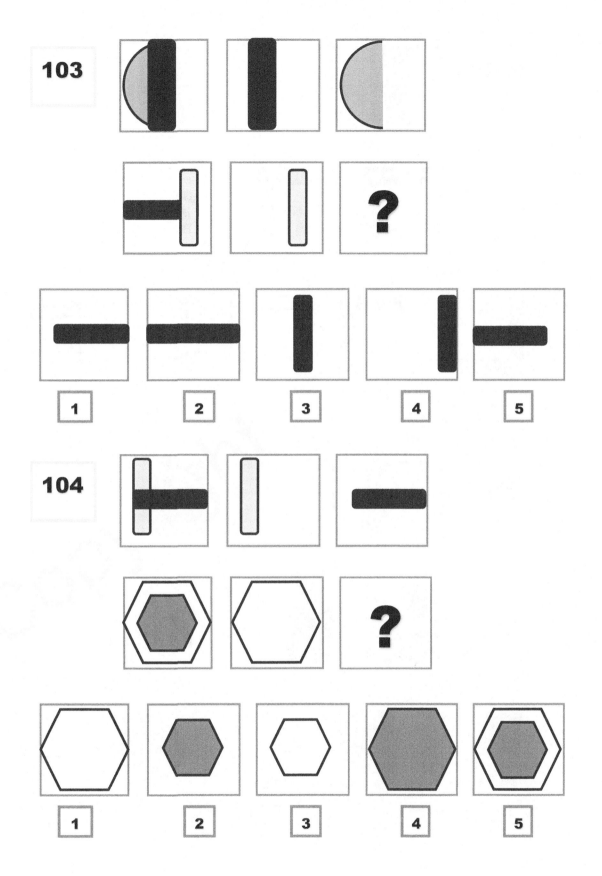

103

104

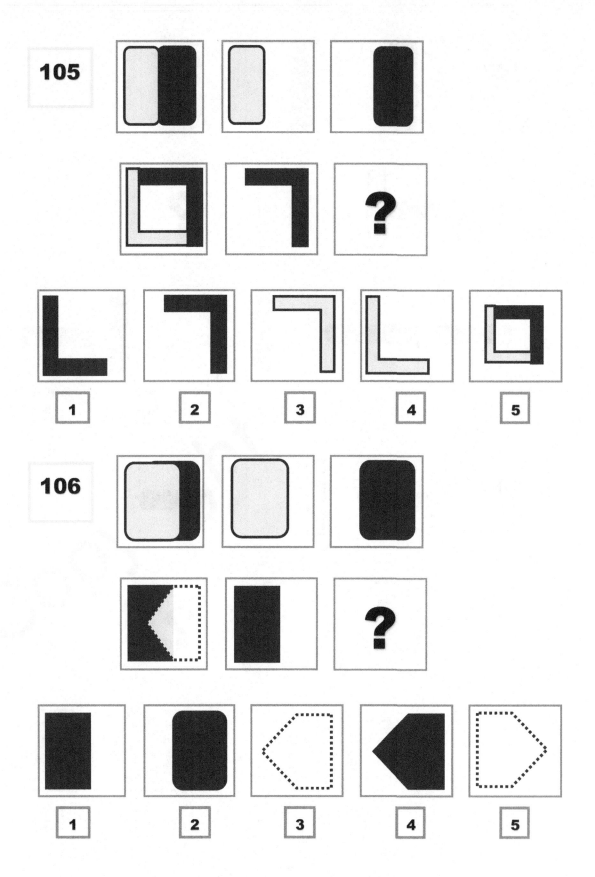

94

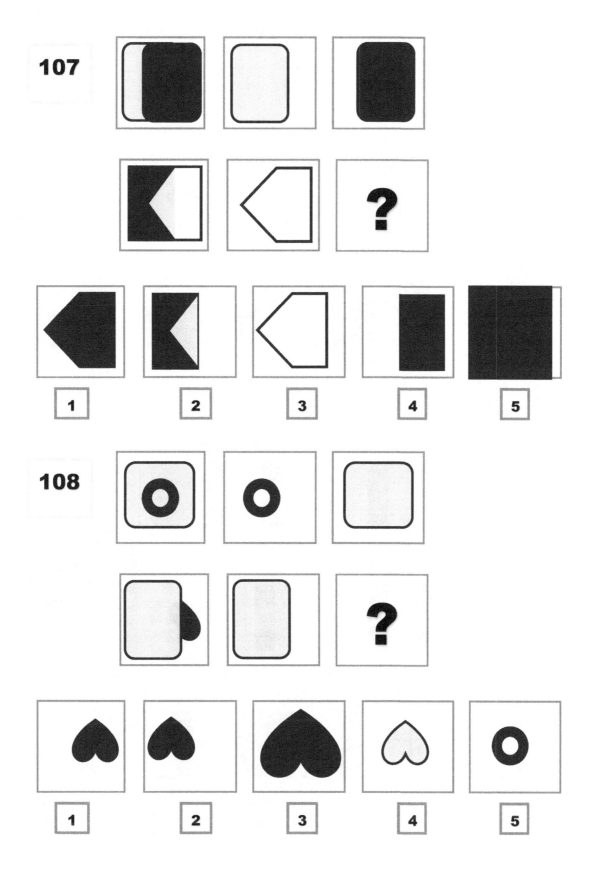

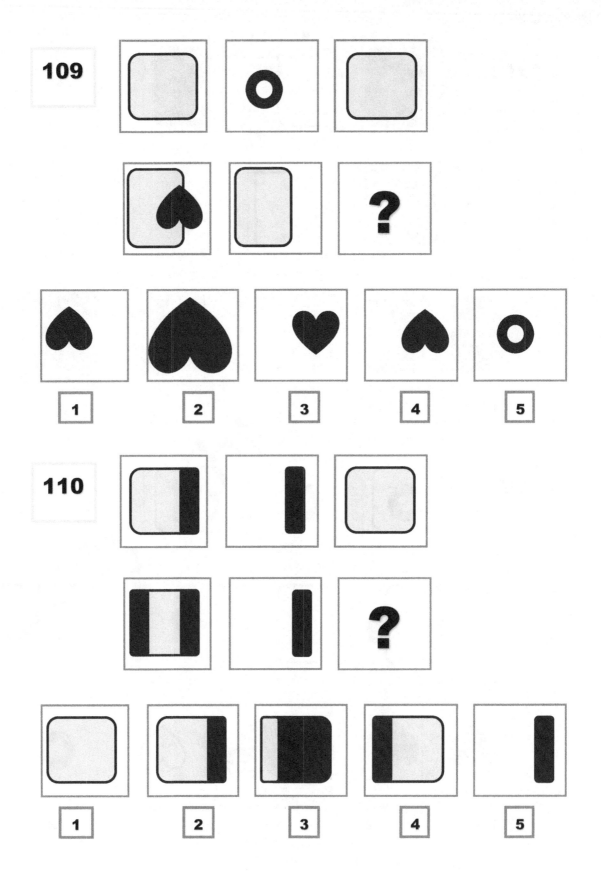

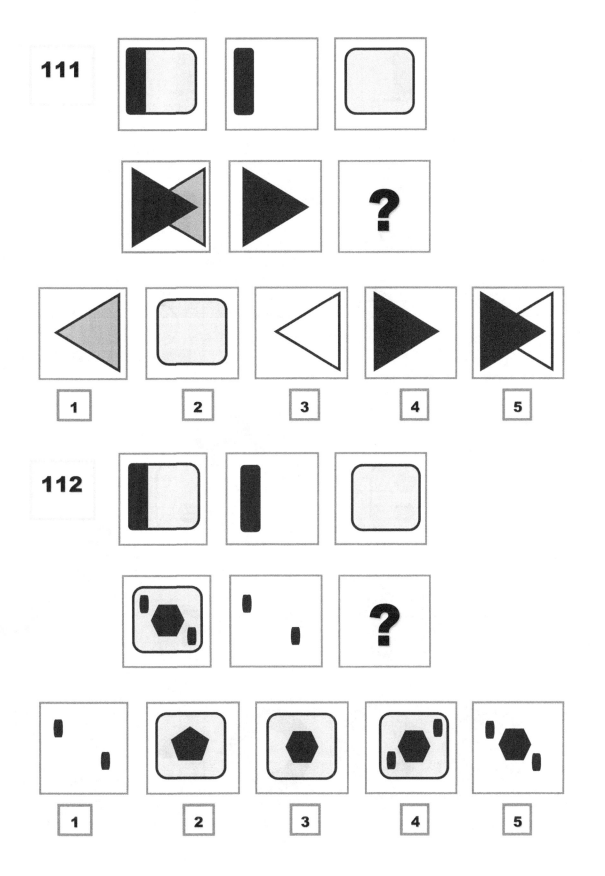

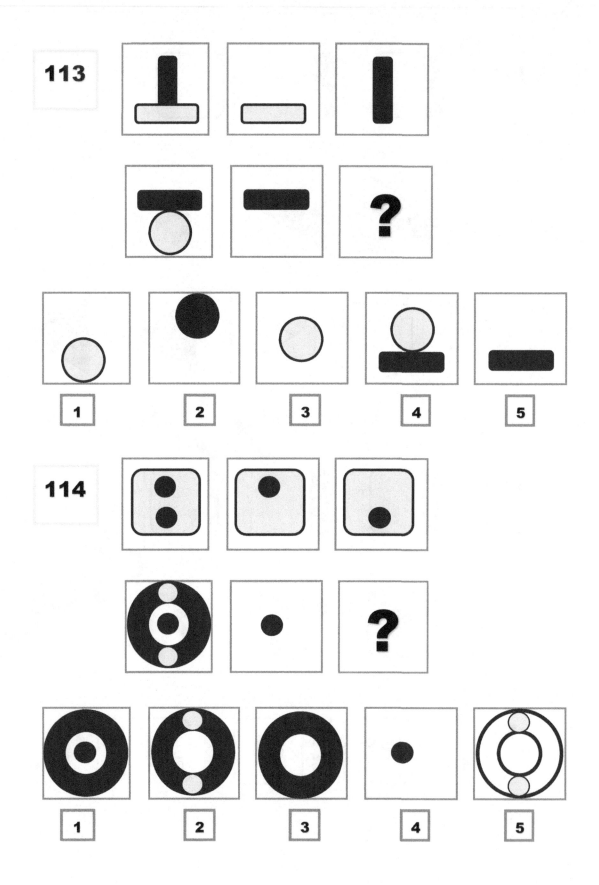

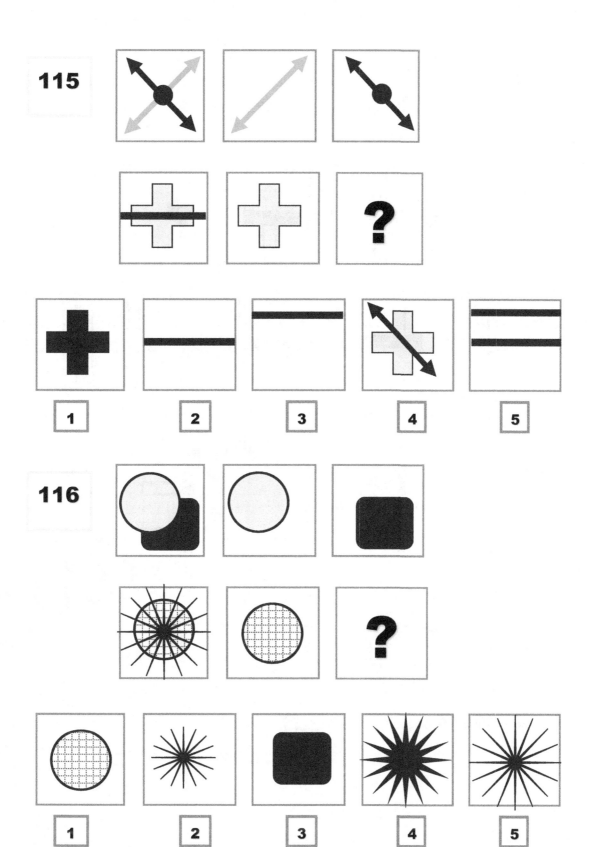

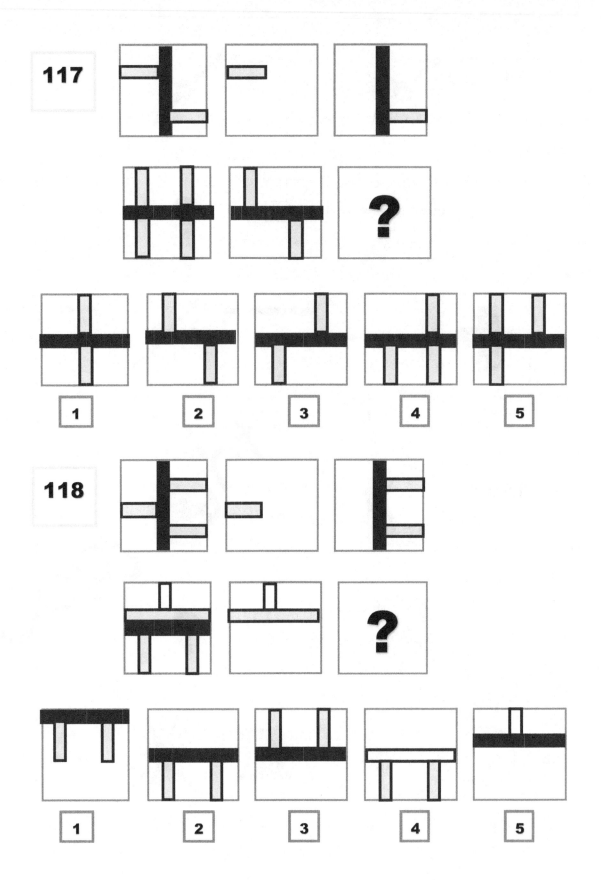

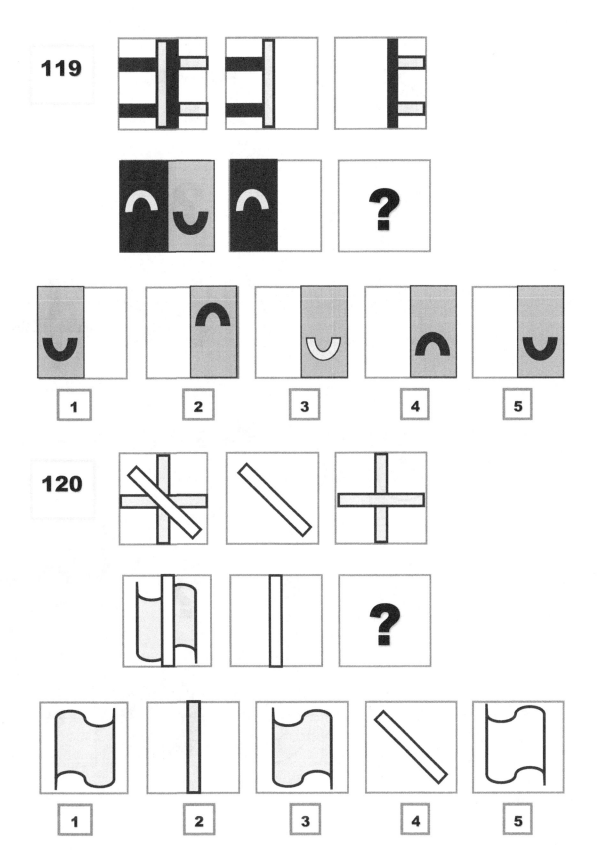

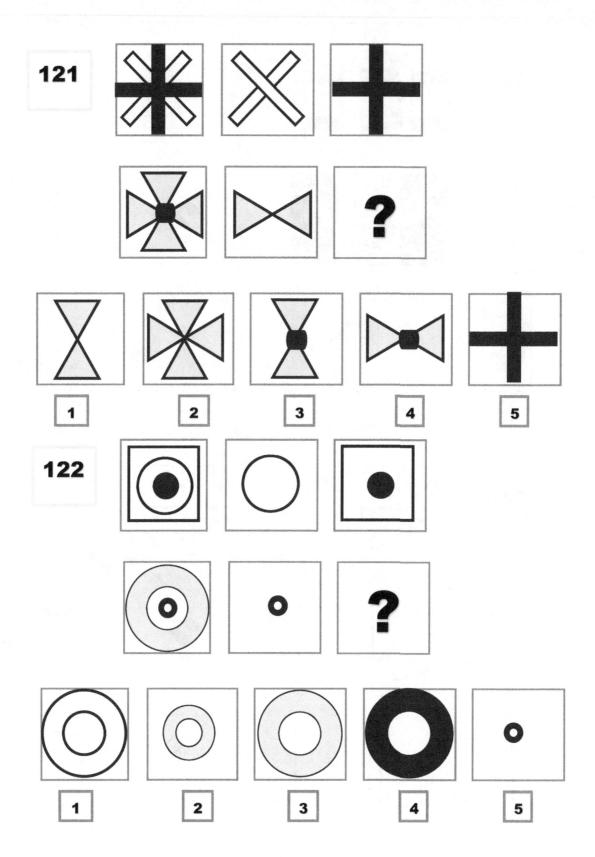

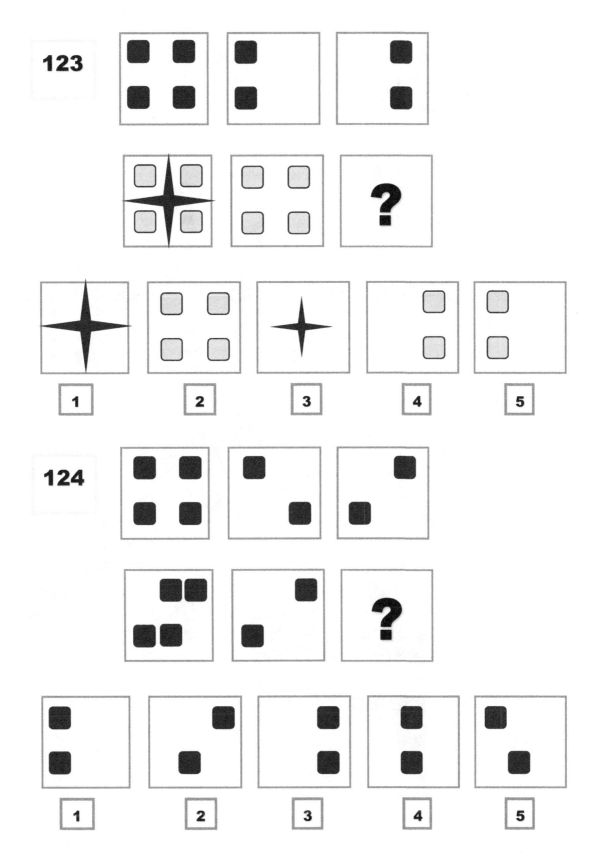

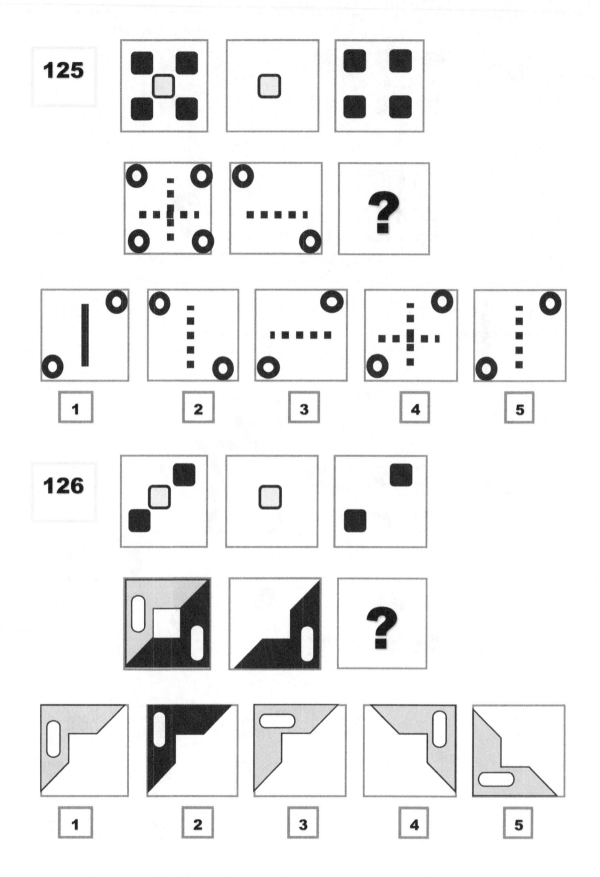

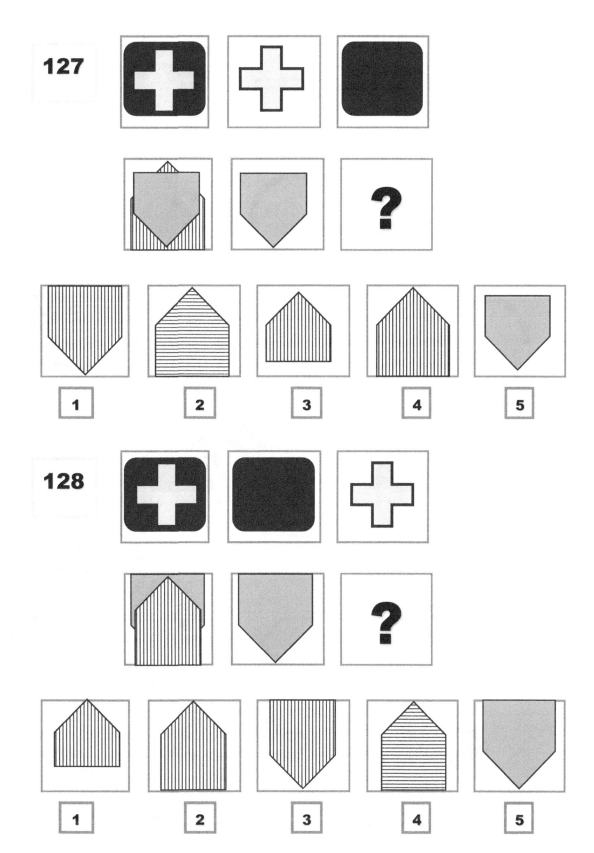

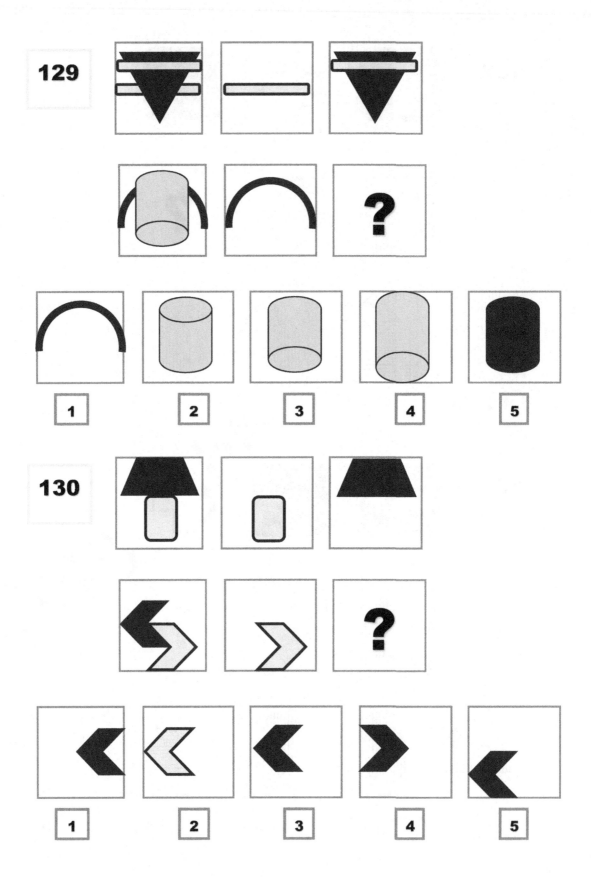

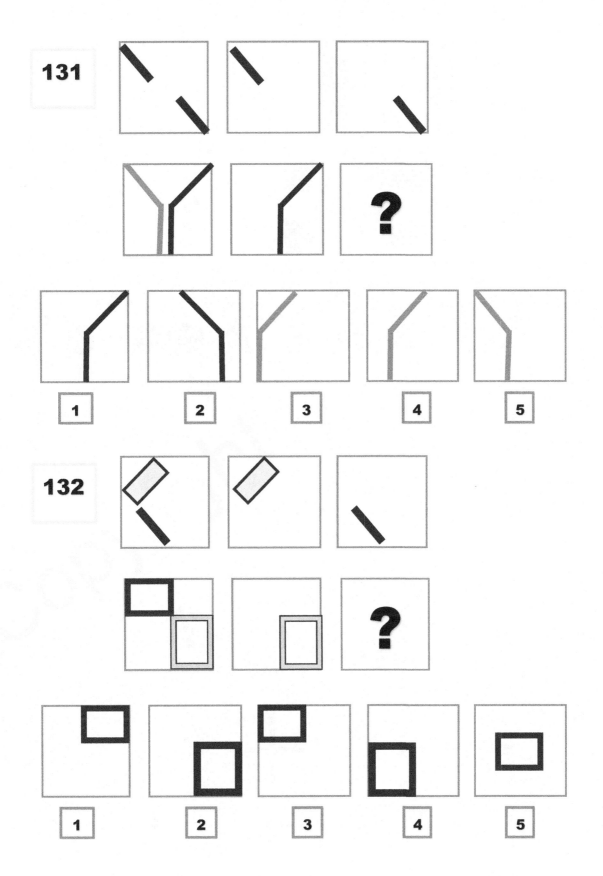

131

132

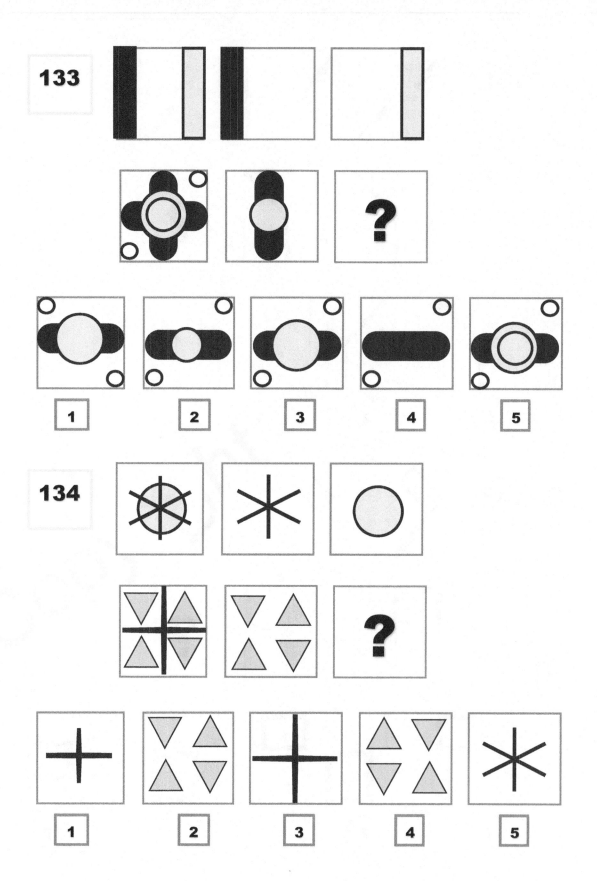

133

134

108

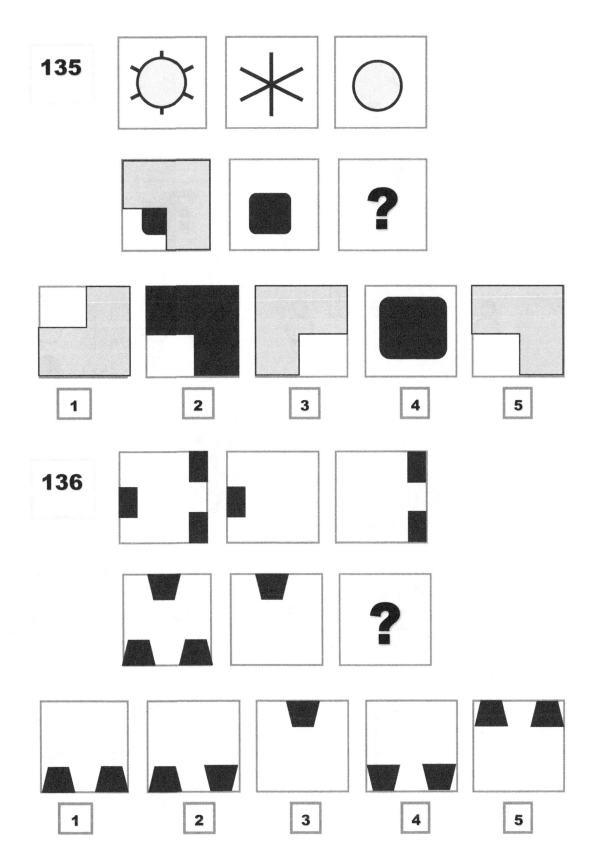

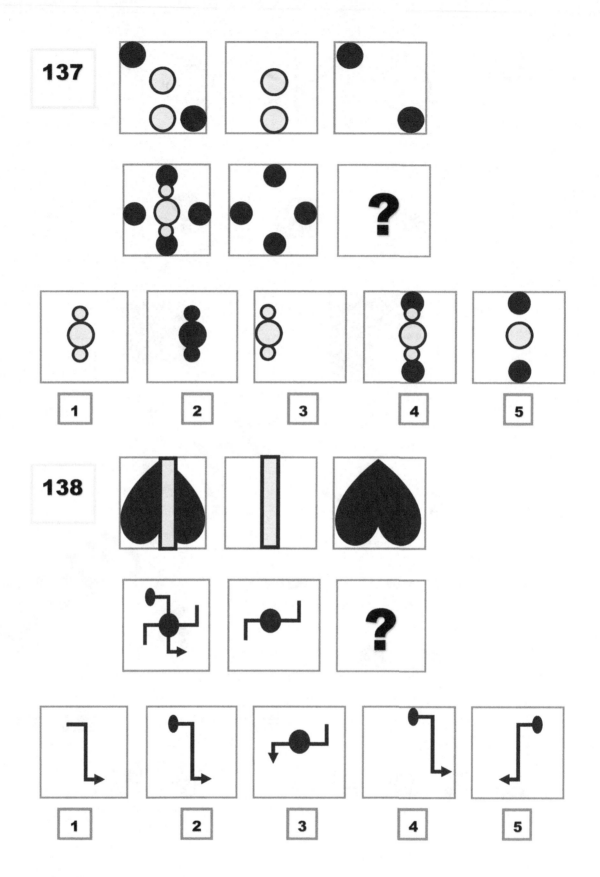

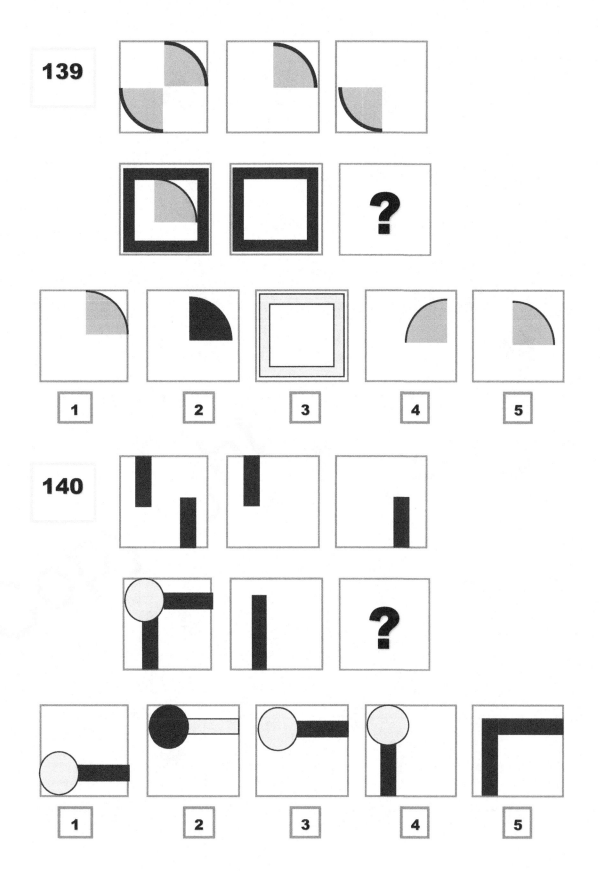

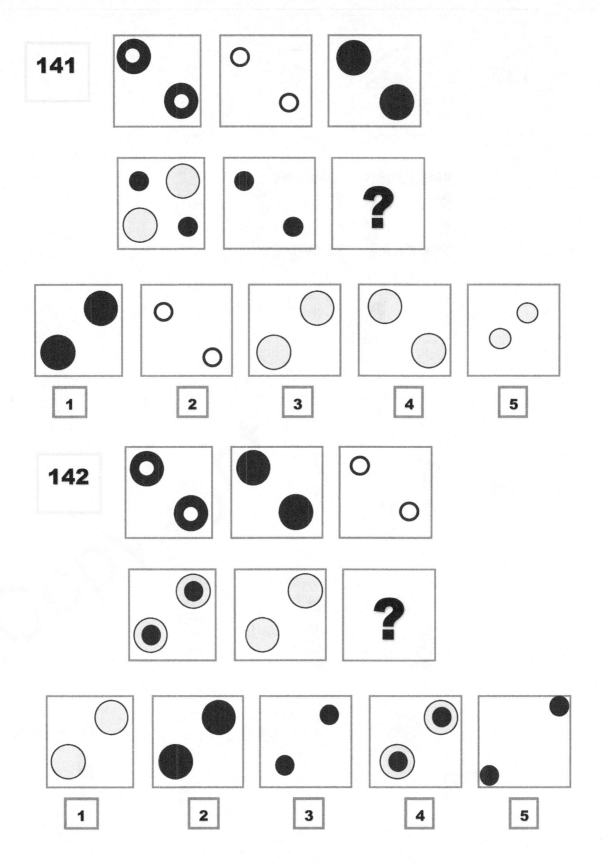

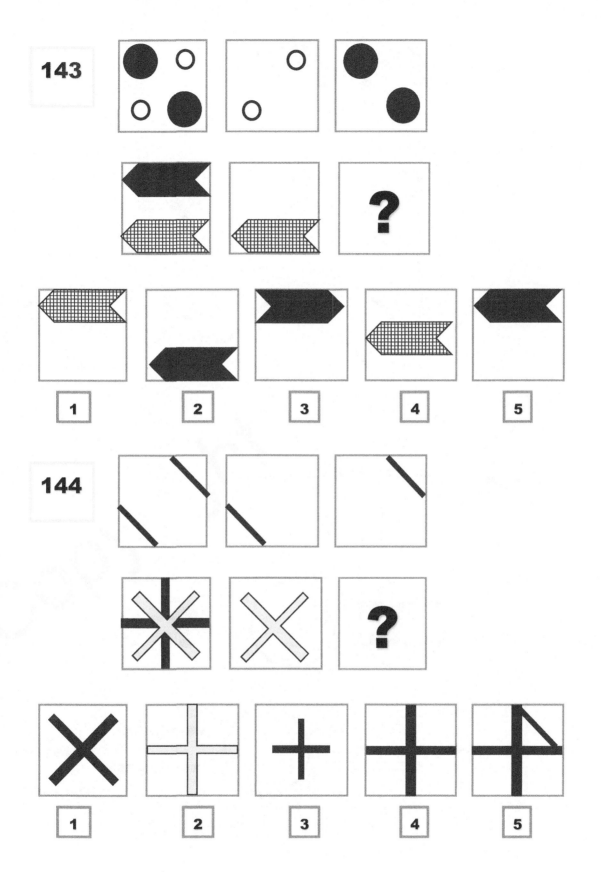

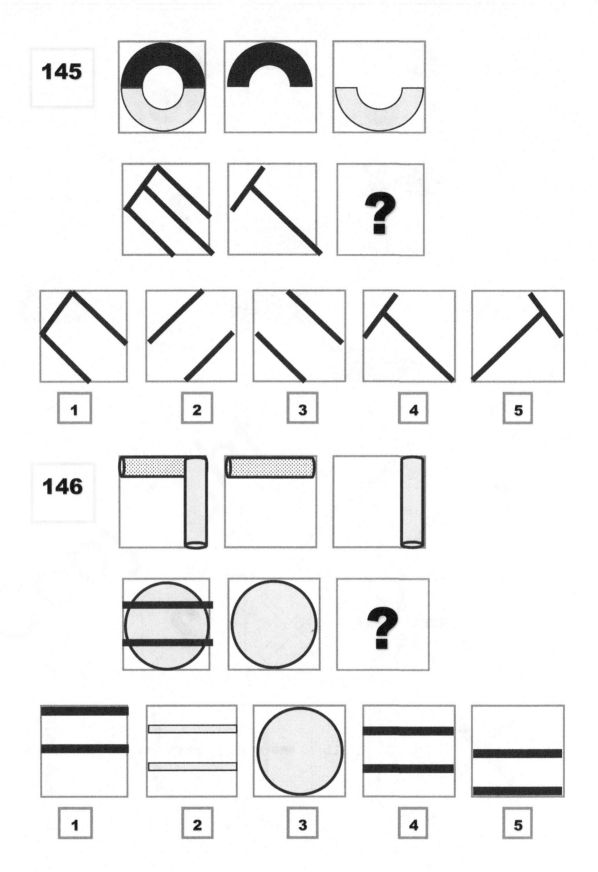

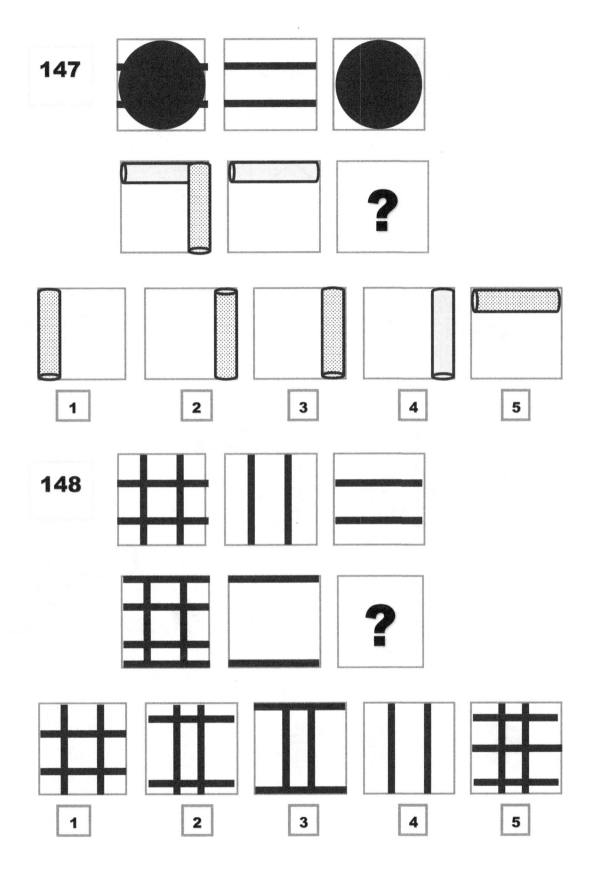

149

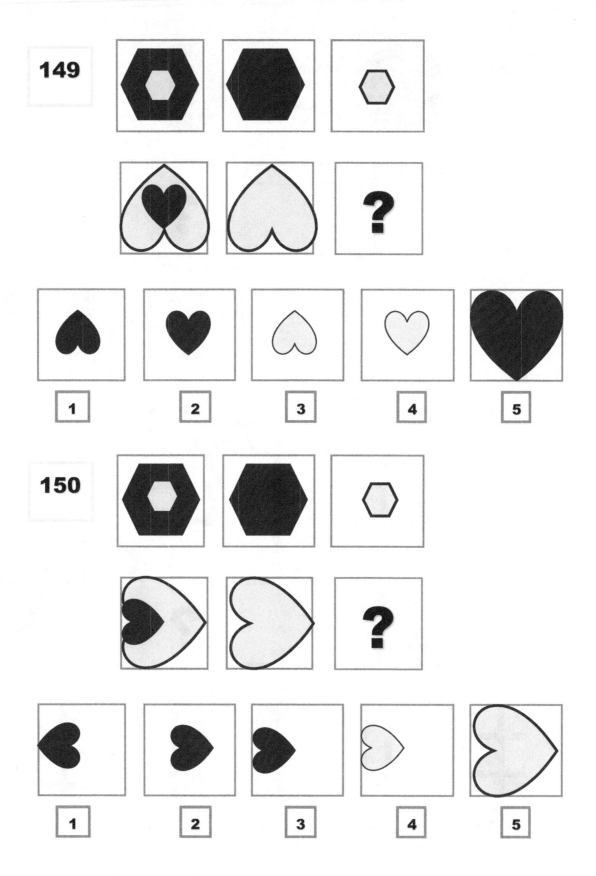

151

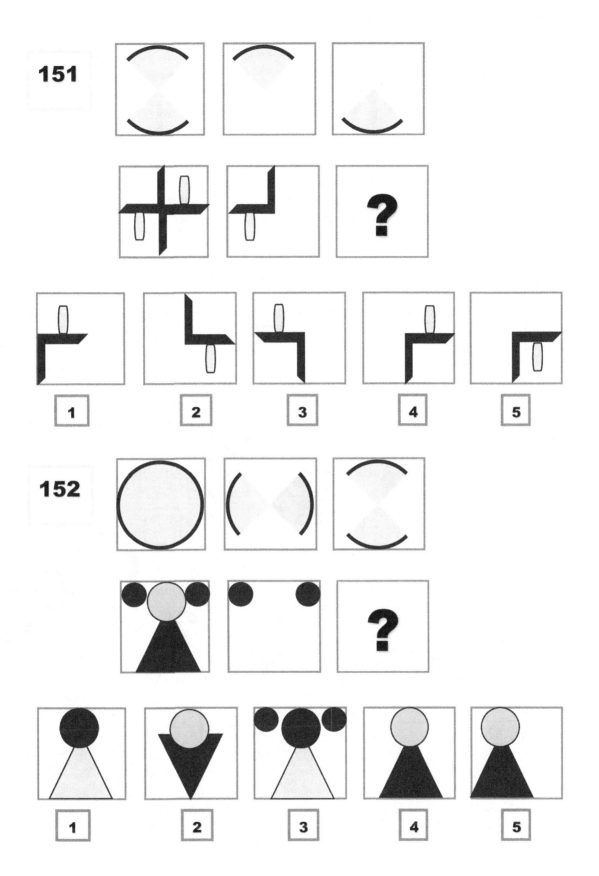

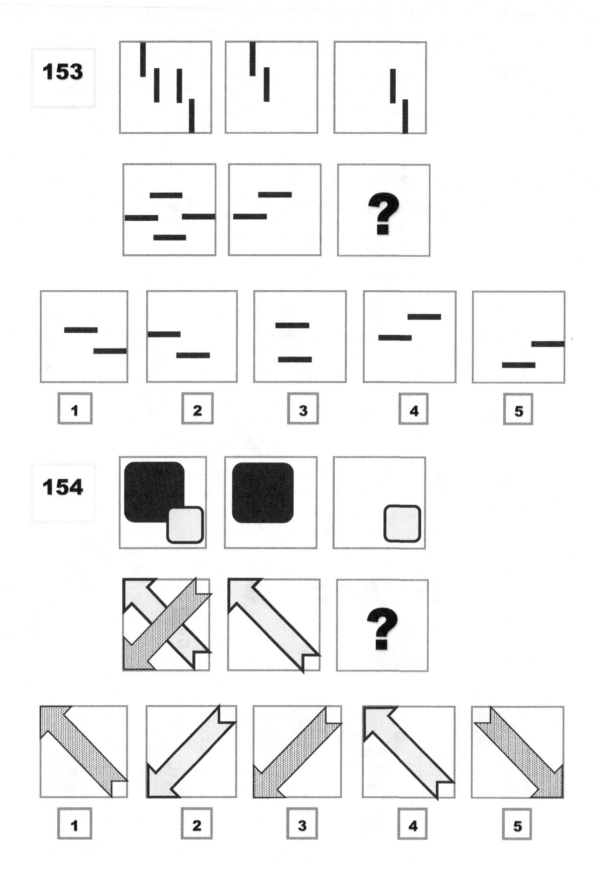

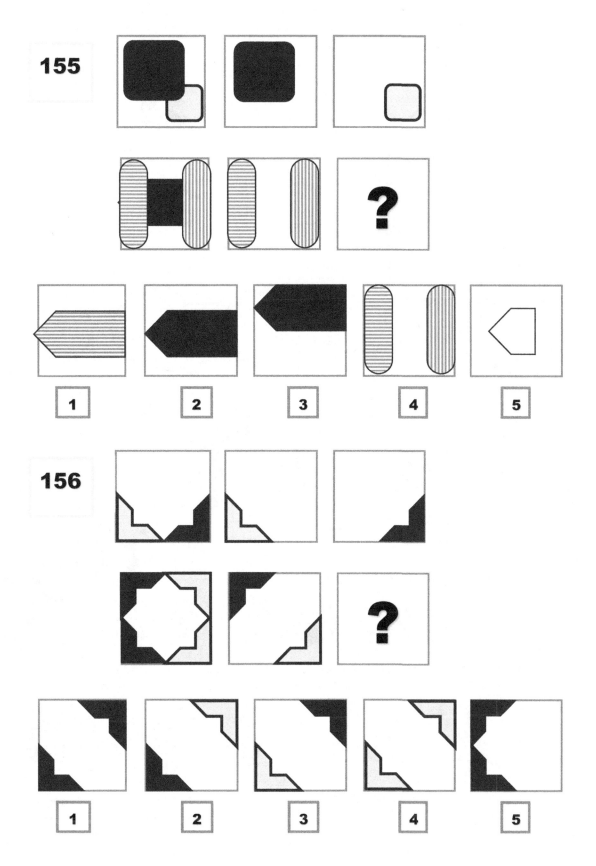

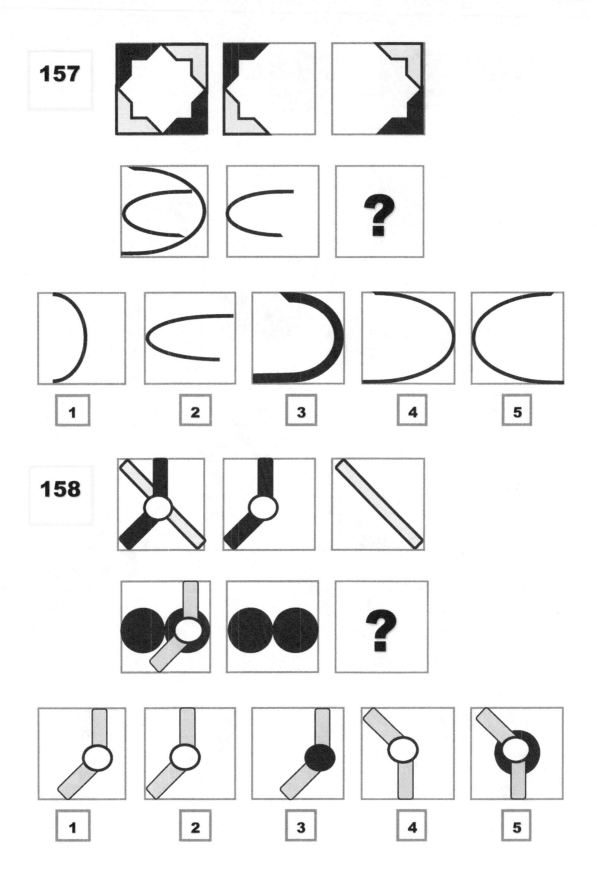

157

158

159

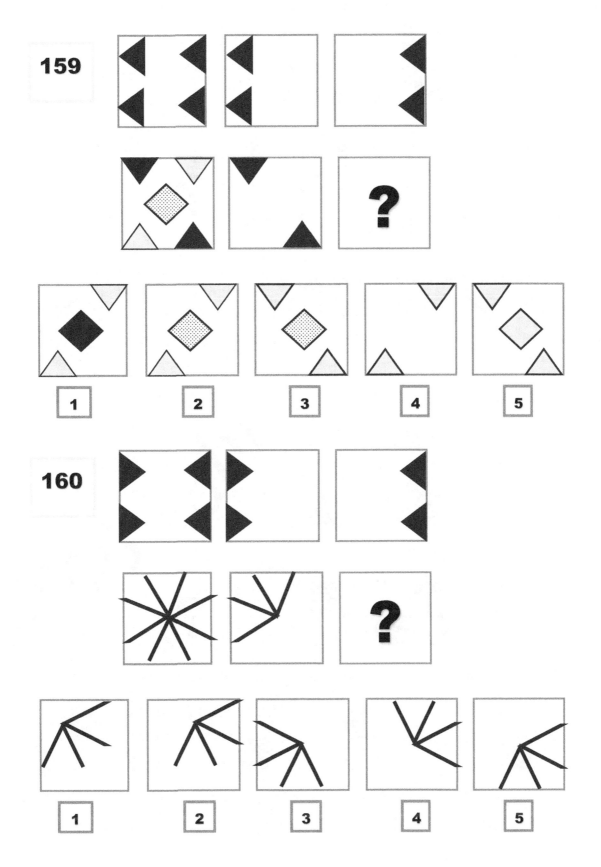

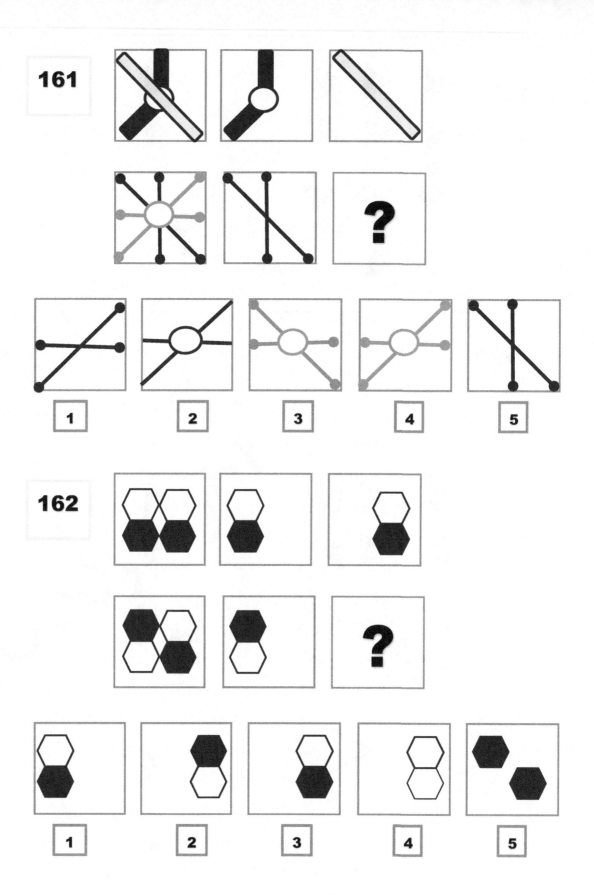

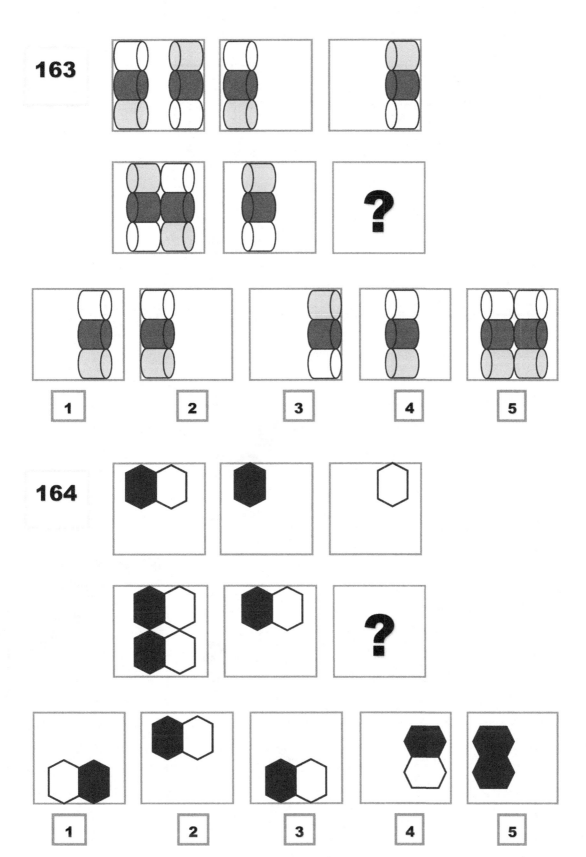

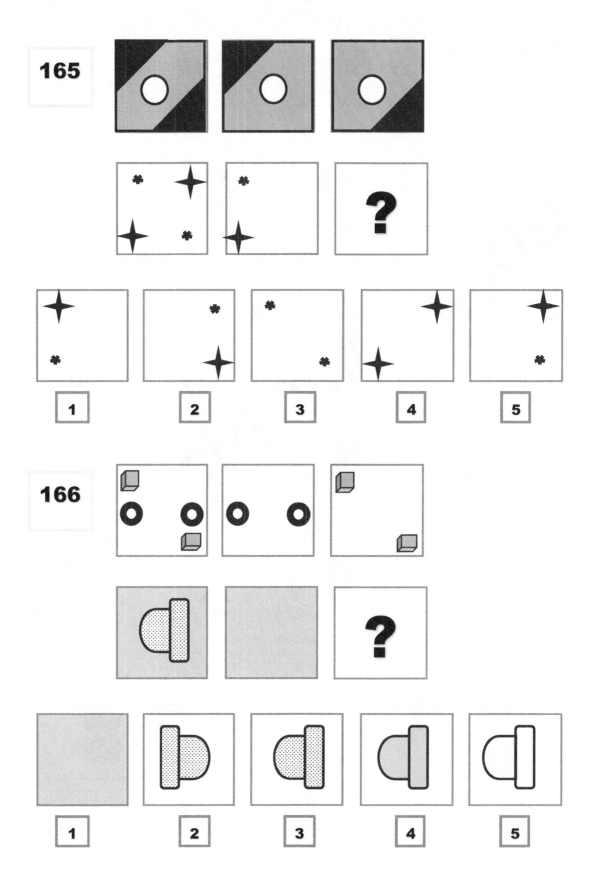

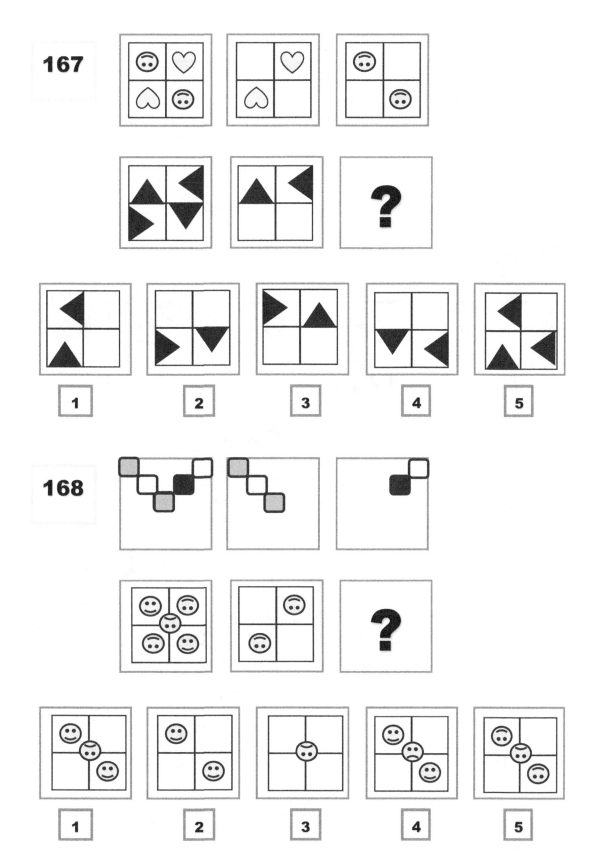

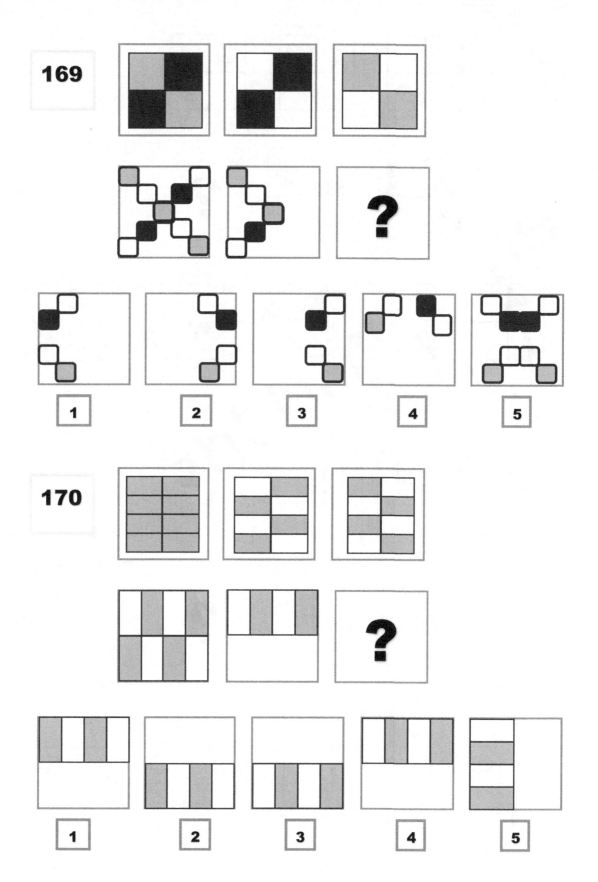

171

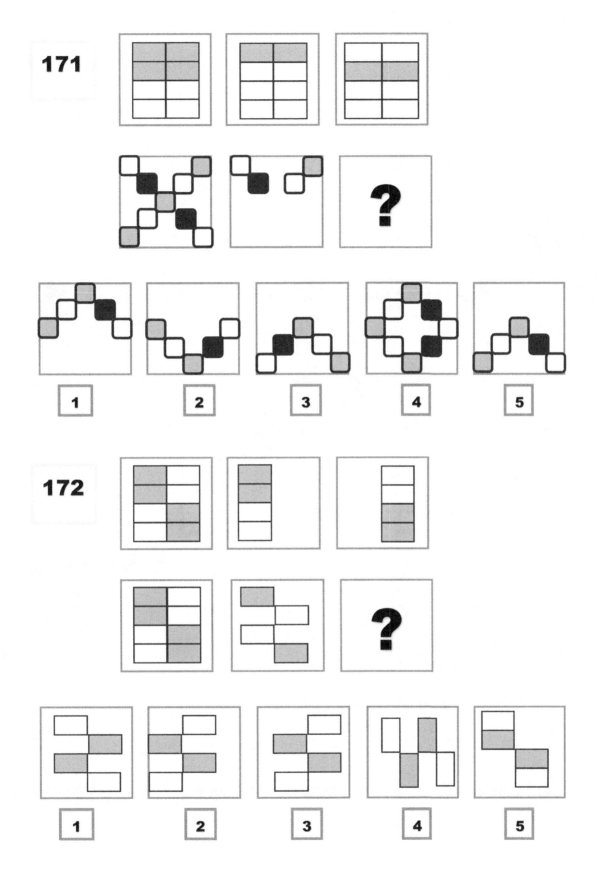

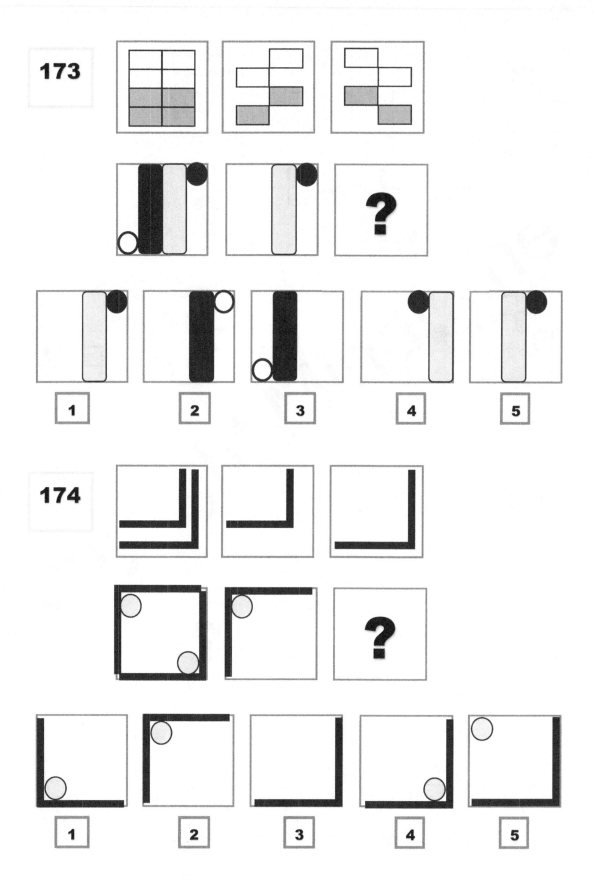

173

174

175

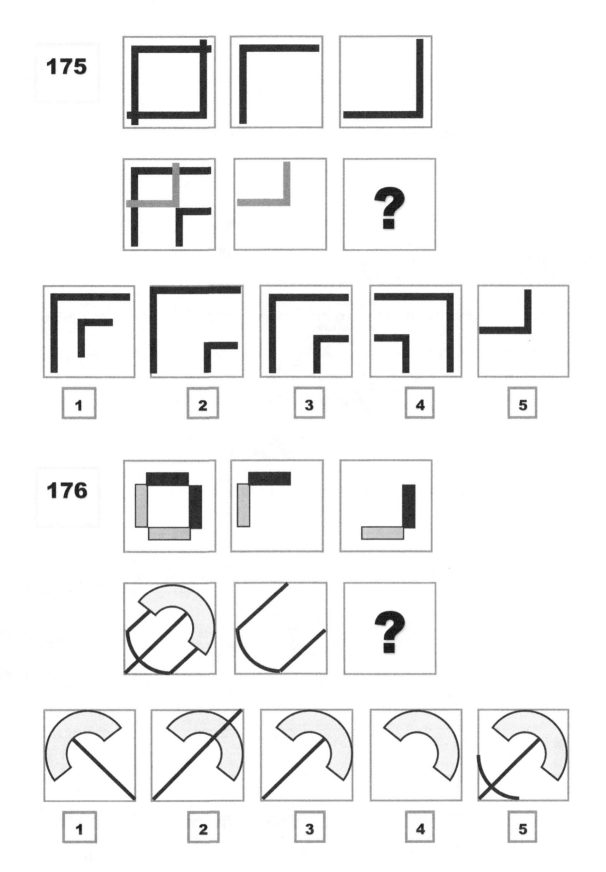

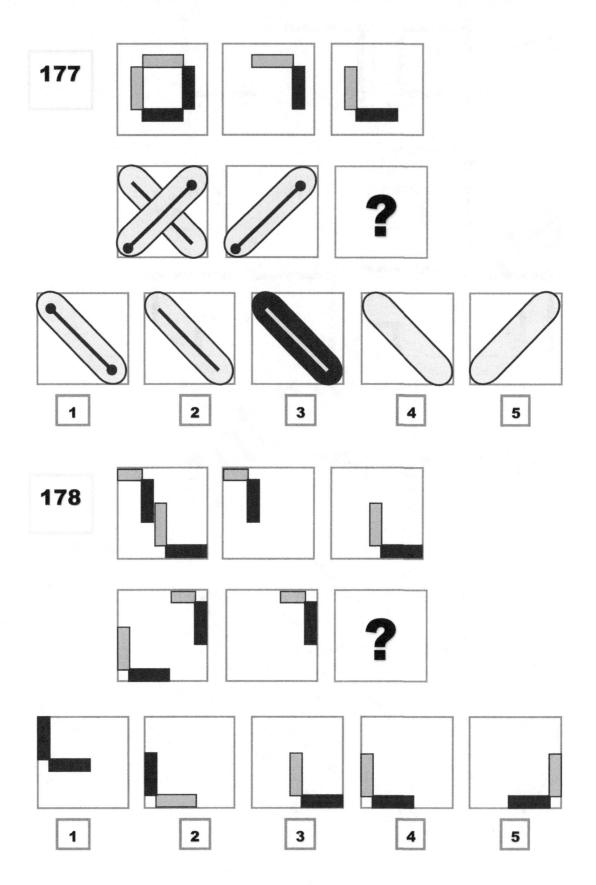

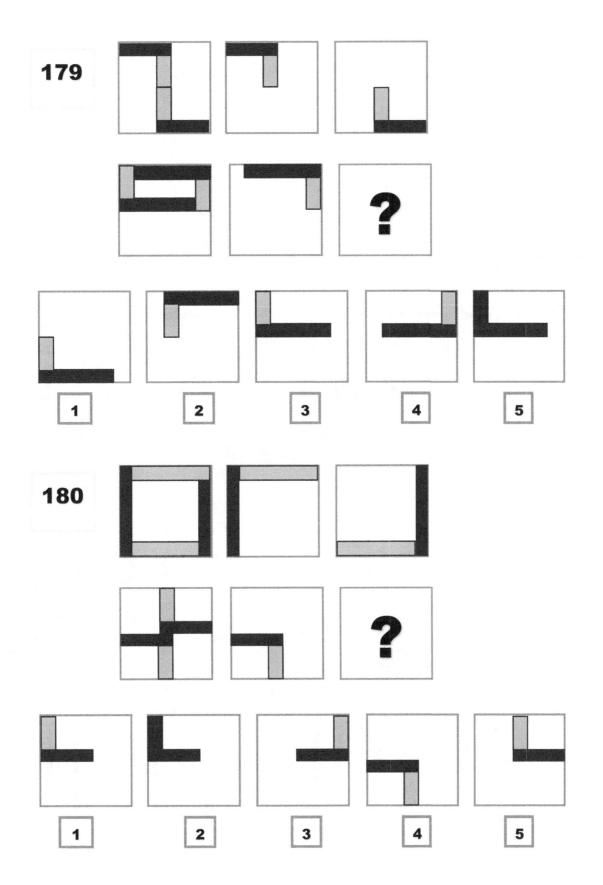

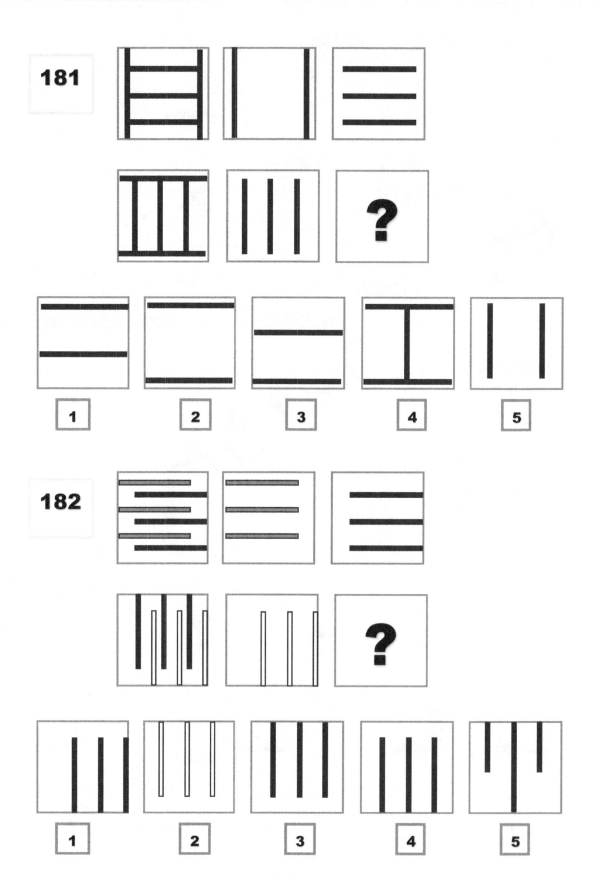

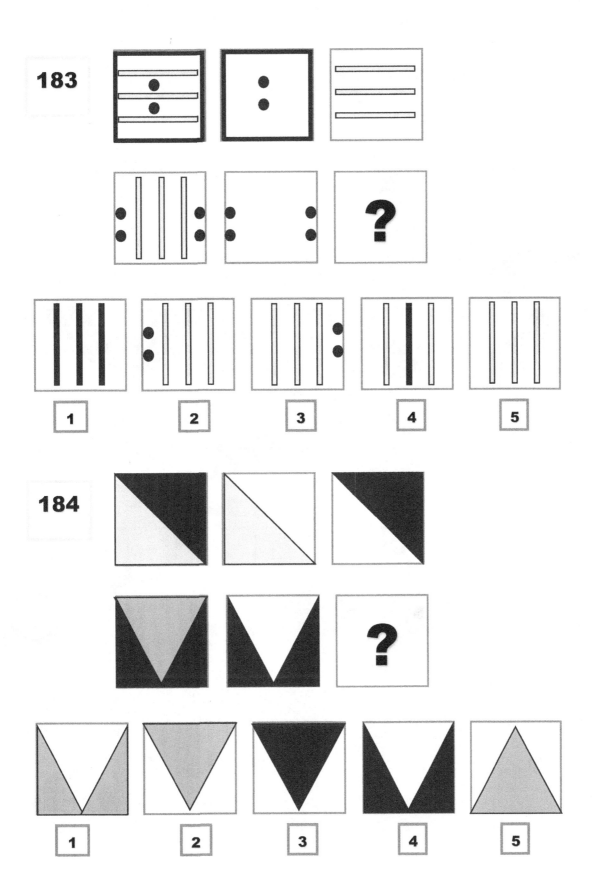

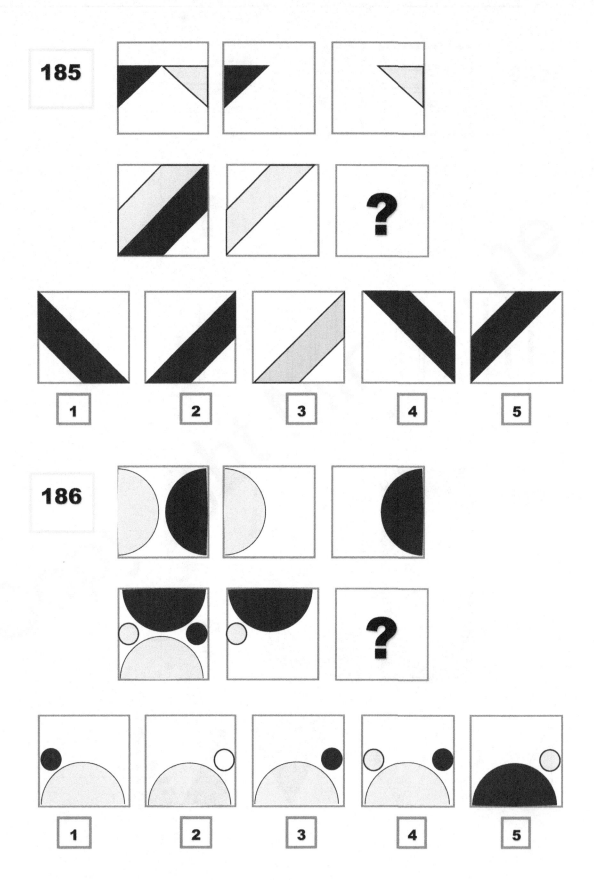

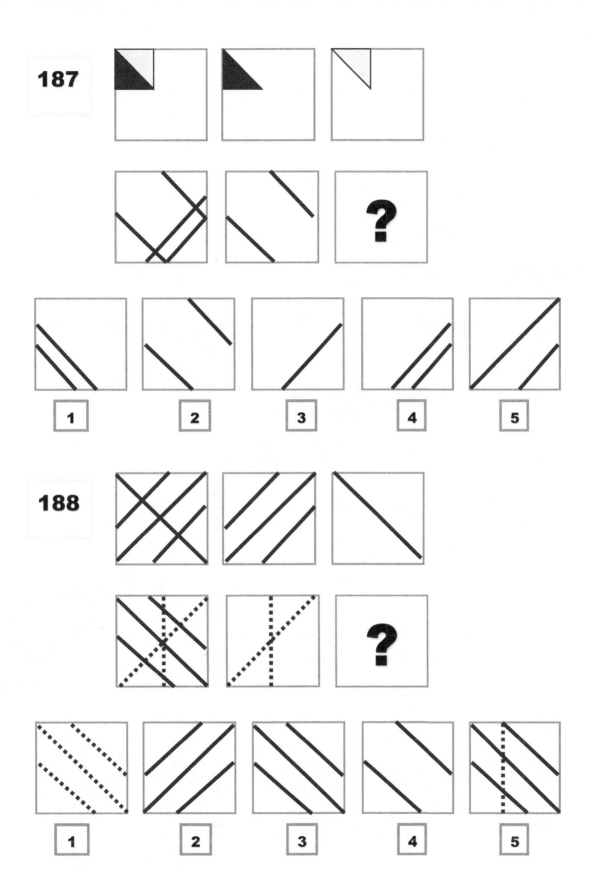

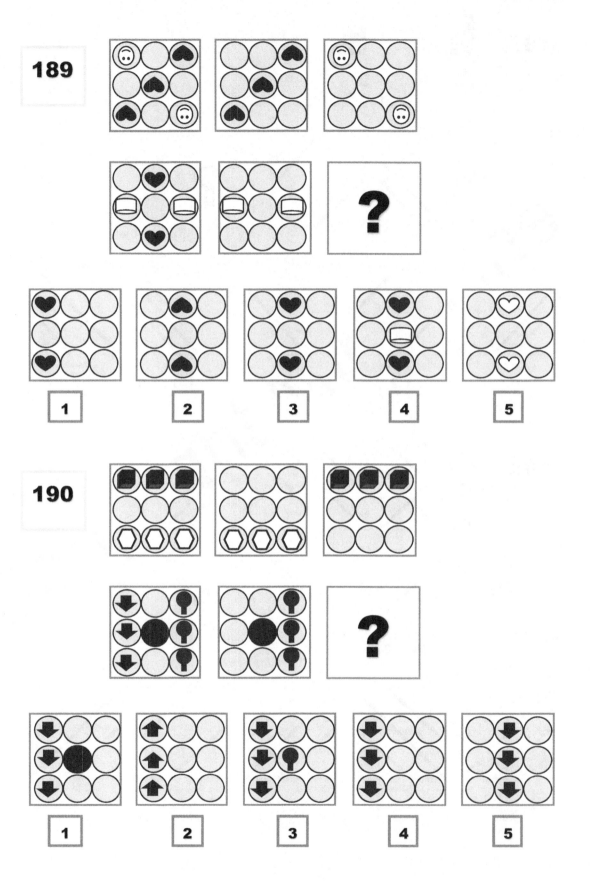

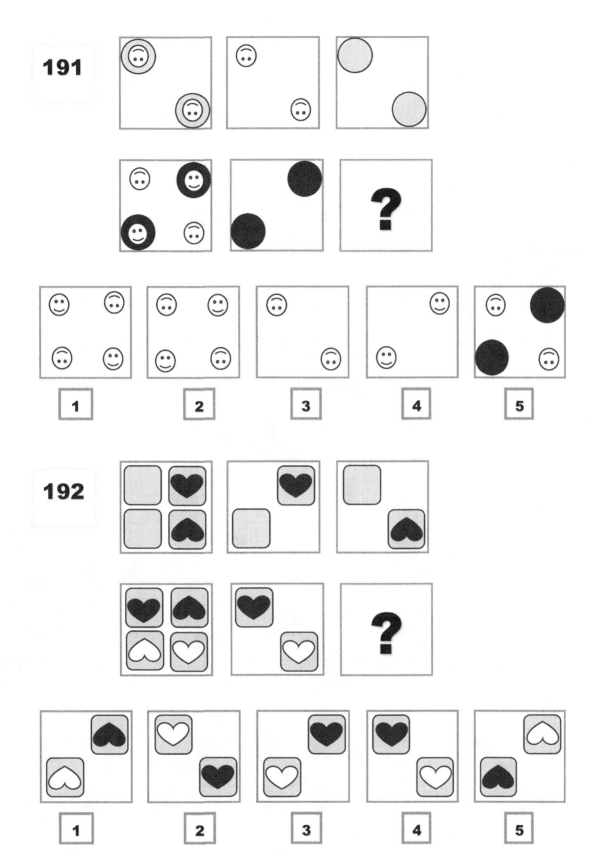

191

192

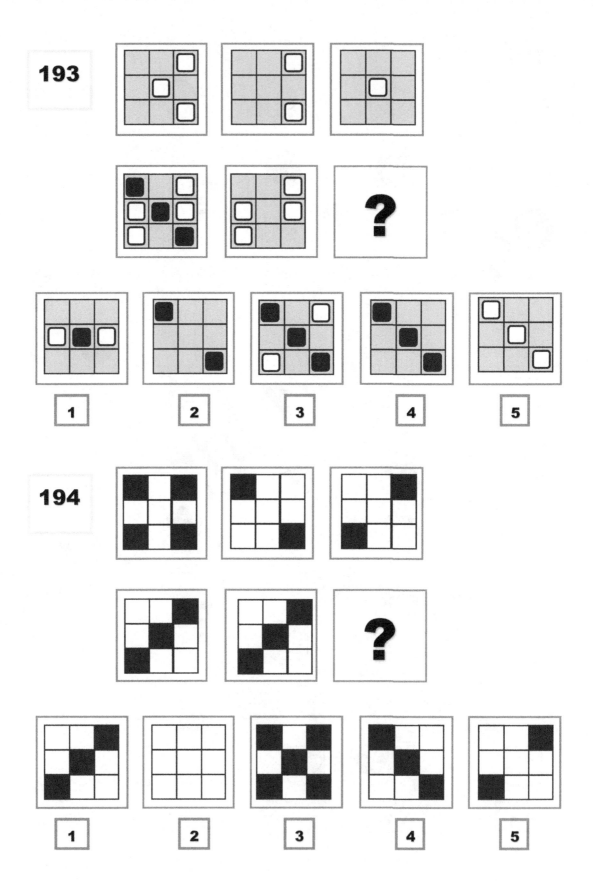

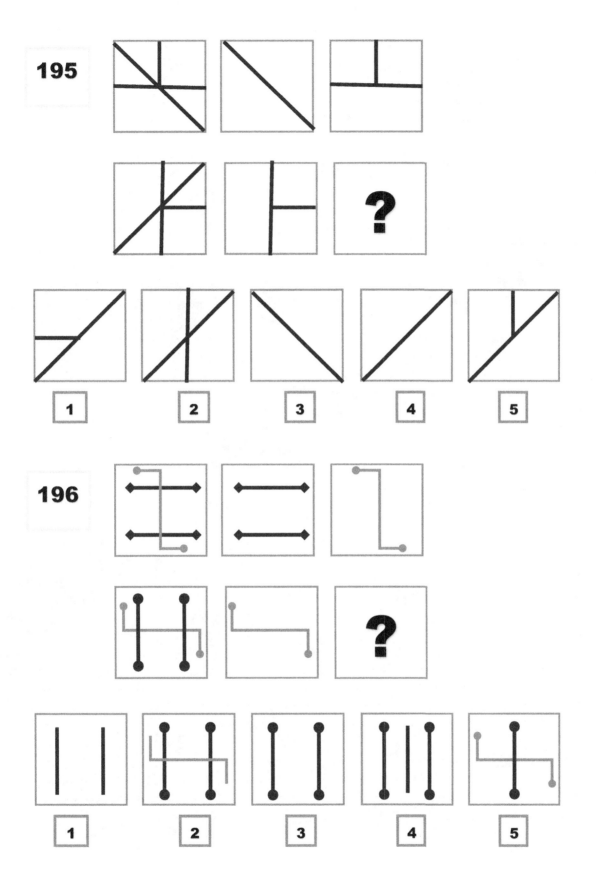

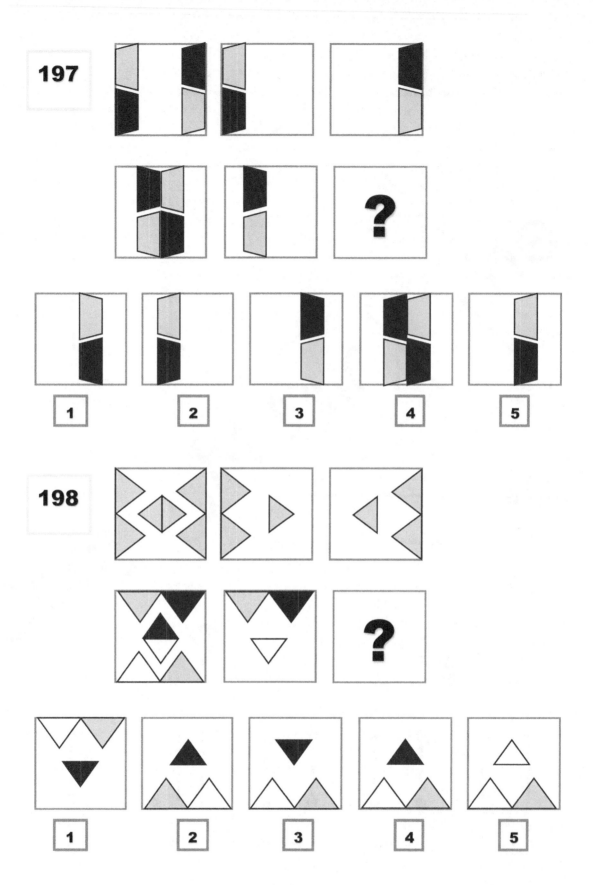

197

198

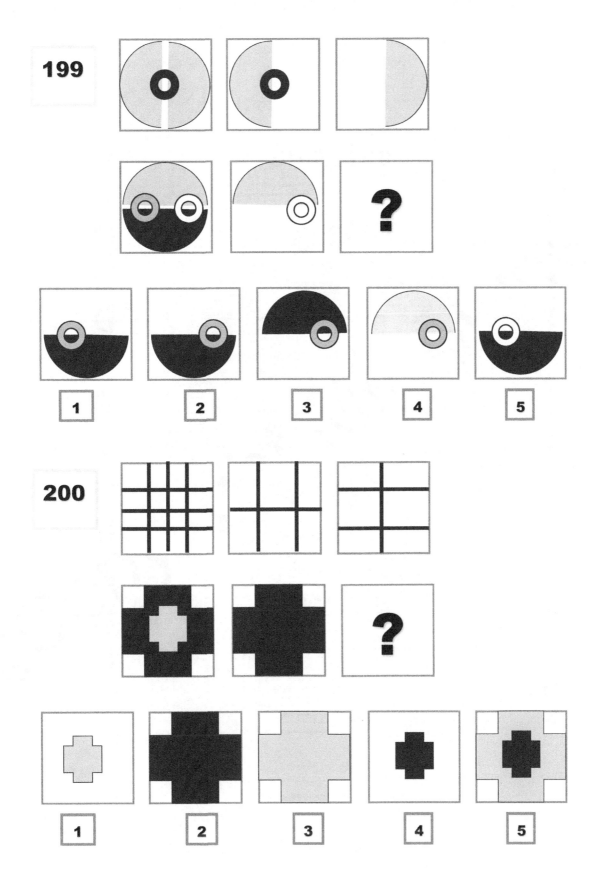

S
P
A
T
I
A
L

V
I
S
U
A
L
I
Z
A
T
I
O
N

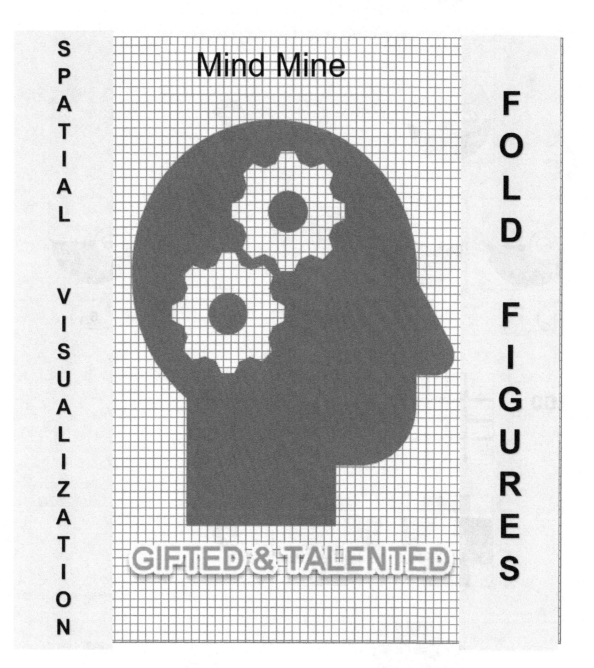

GIFTED & TALENTED

F
O
L
D

F
I
G
U
R
E
S

201

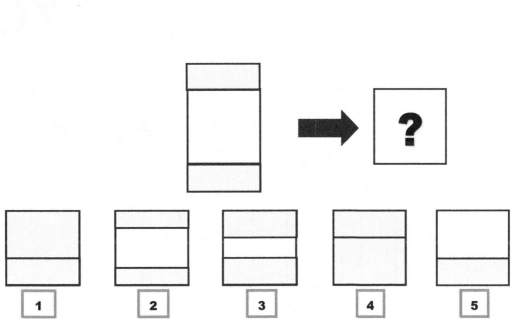

202

203

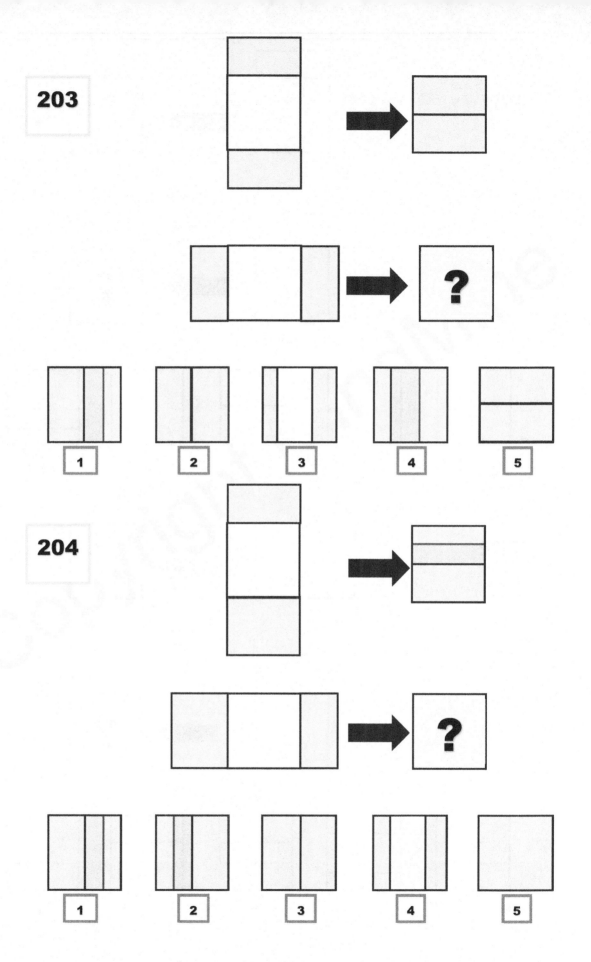

204

205

206

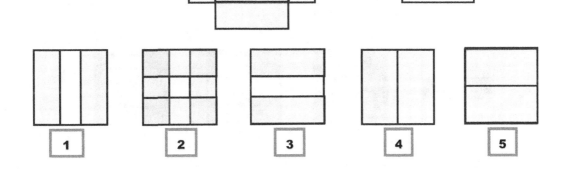

145

207

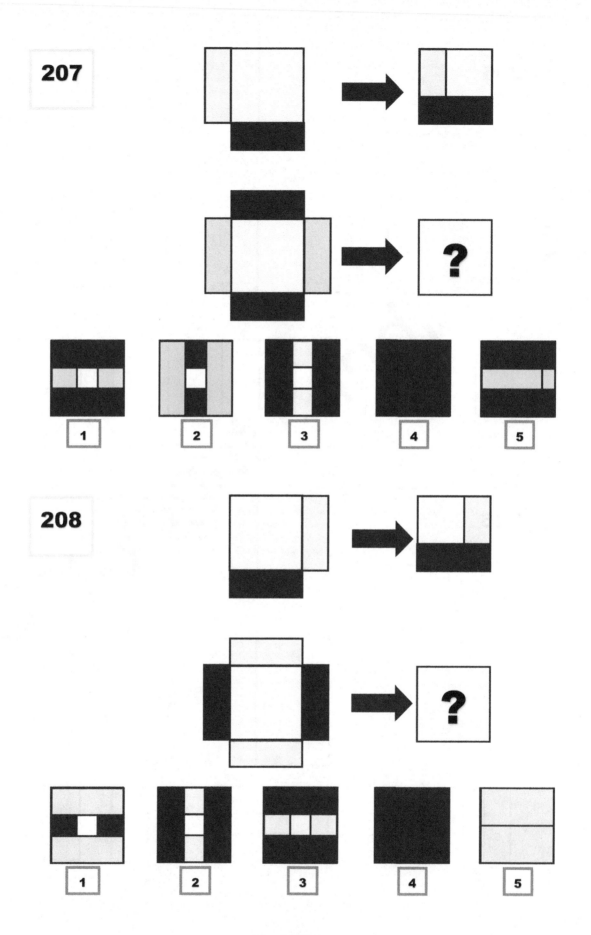

209

210

1 2 3 4 5

1 2 3 4 5

211

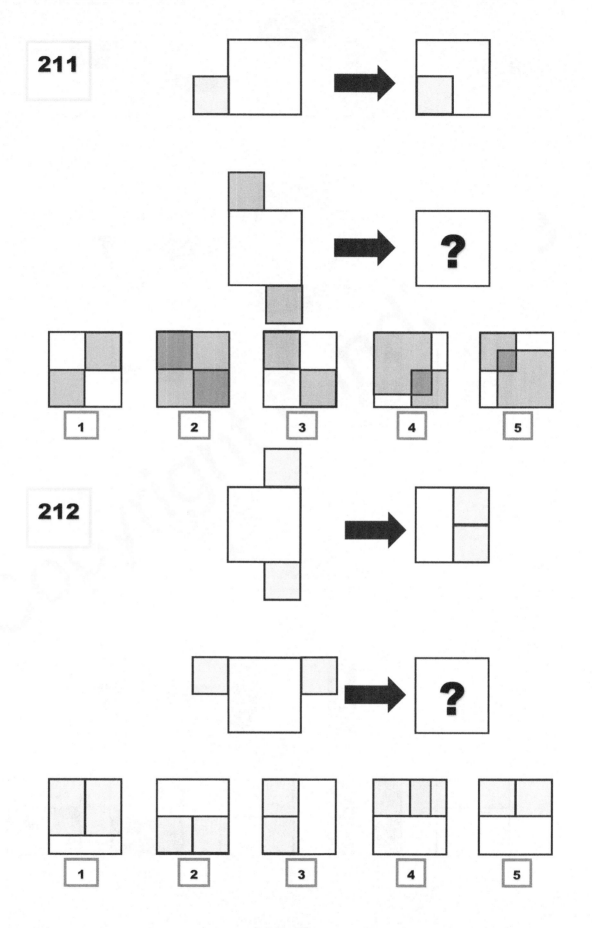

212

213

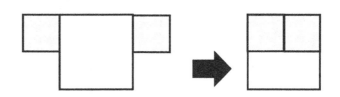

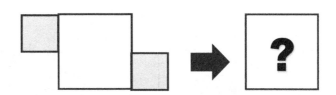

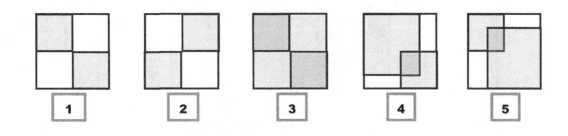

214

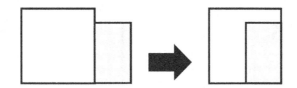

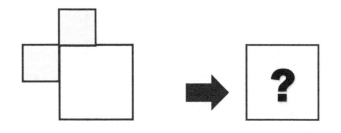

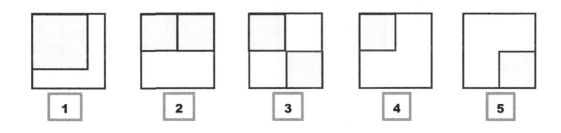

149

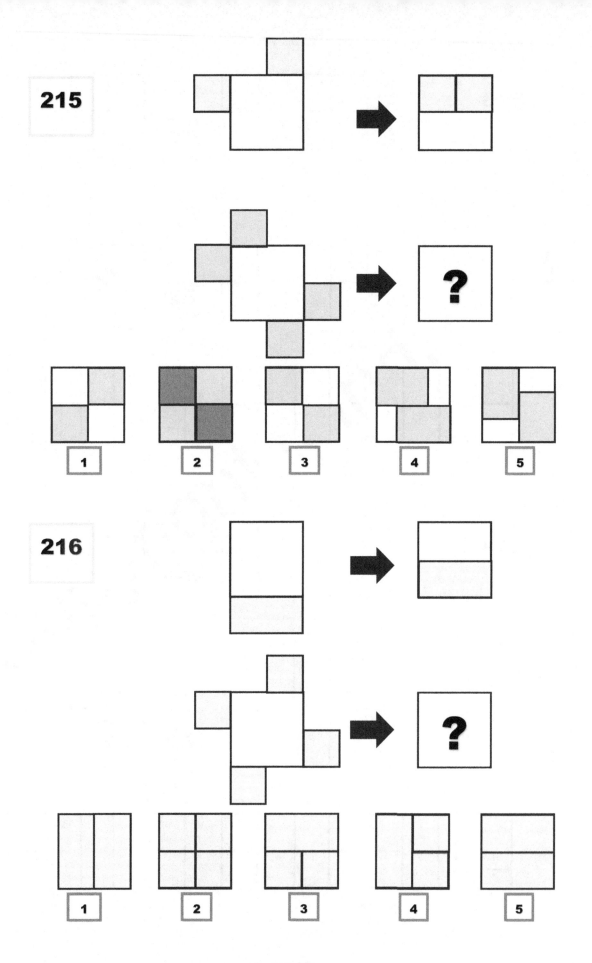

217

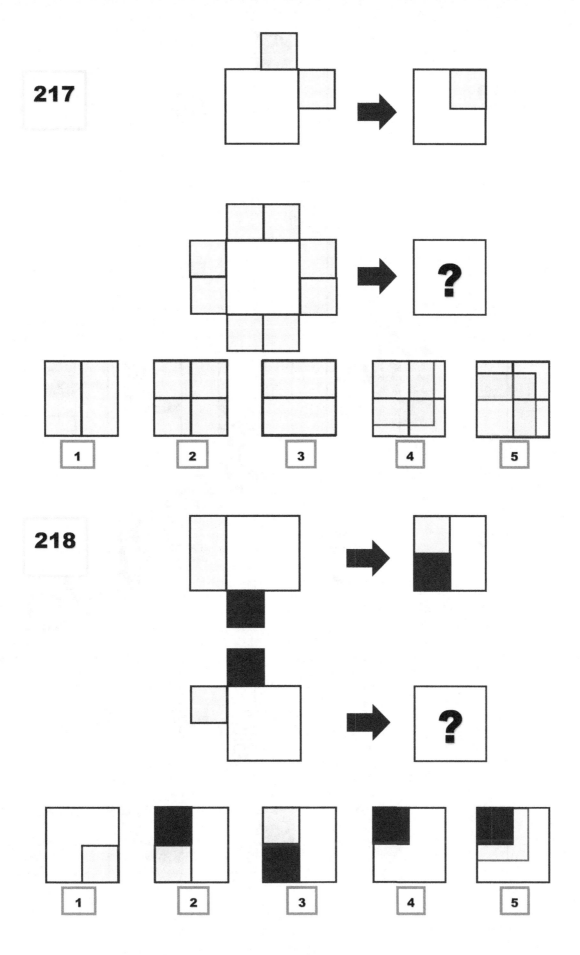

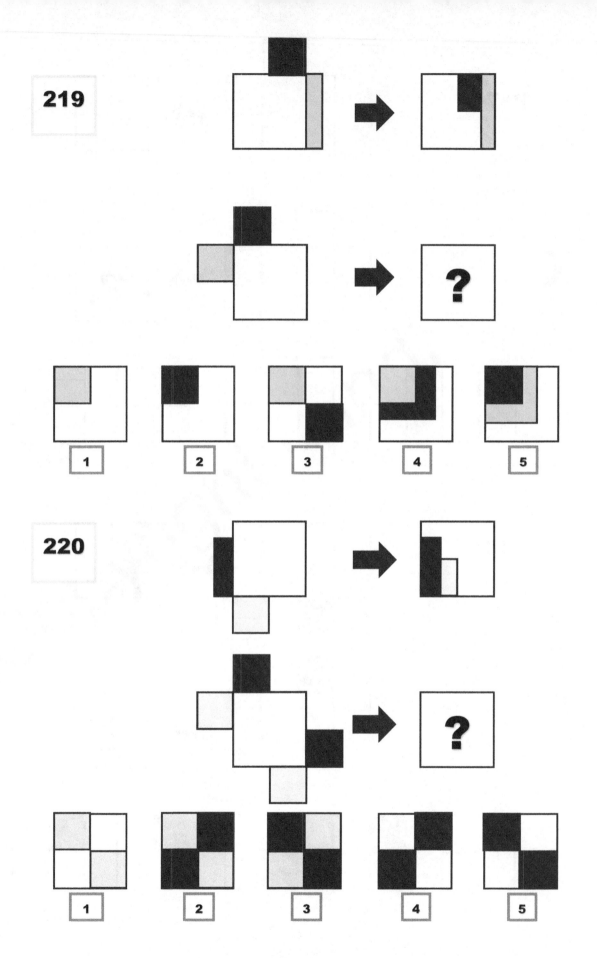

219

220

152

221

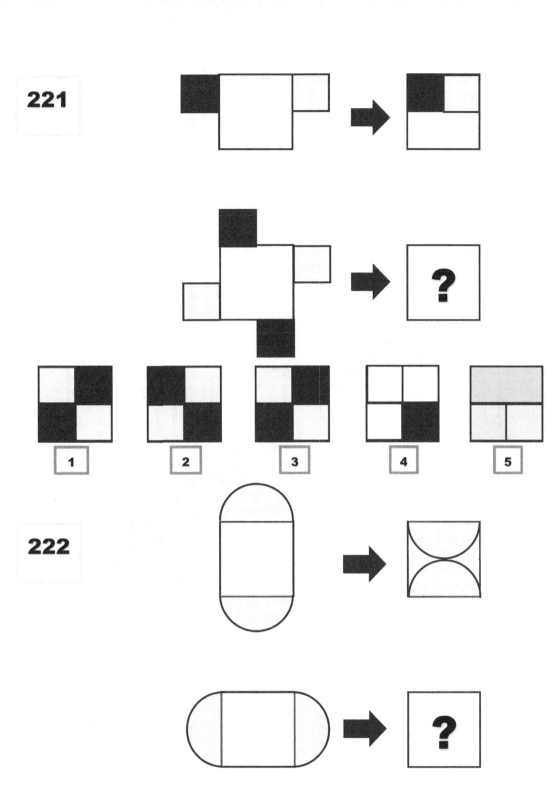

222

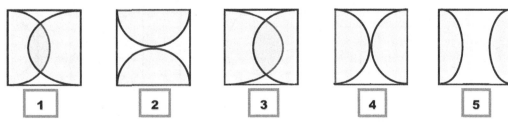

153

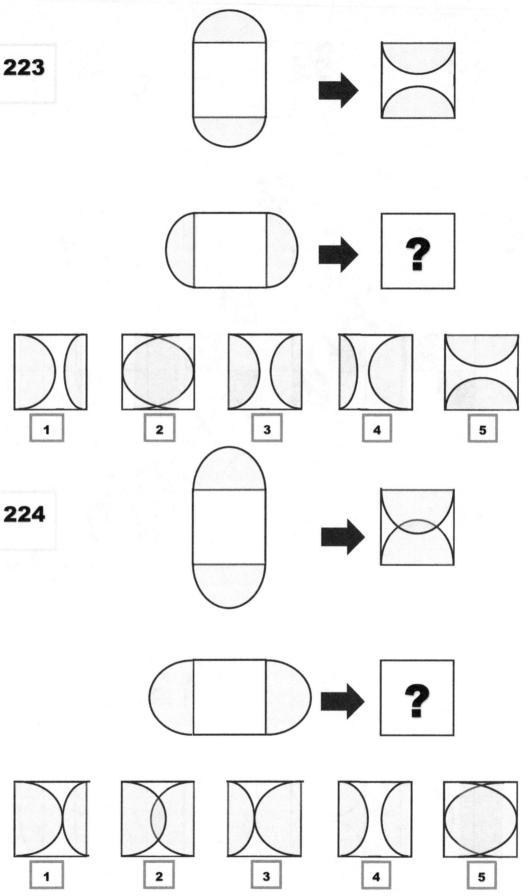

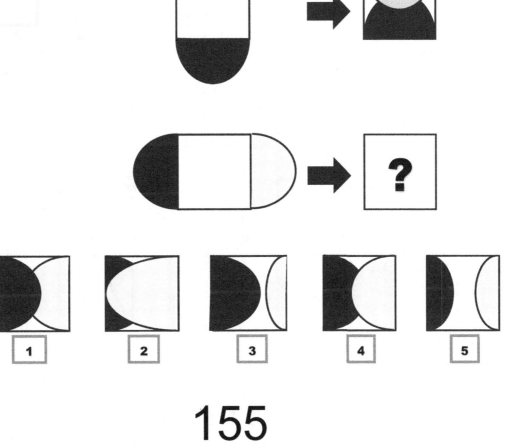

227

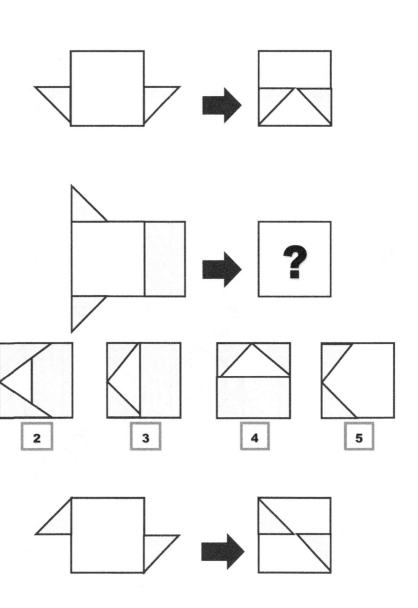

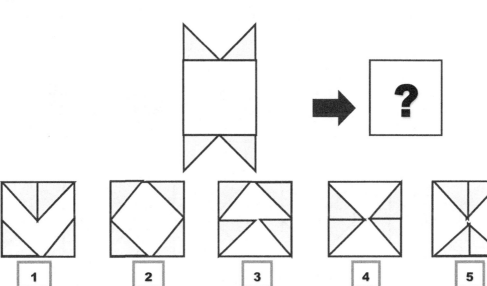

231

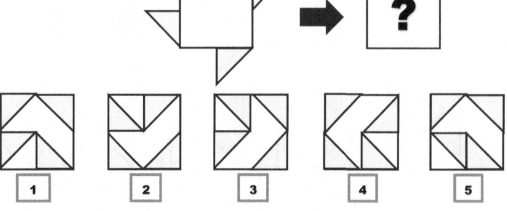

232

158

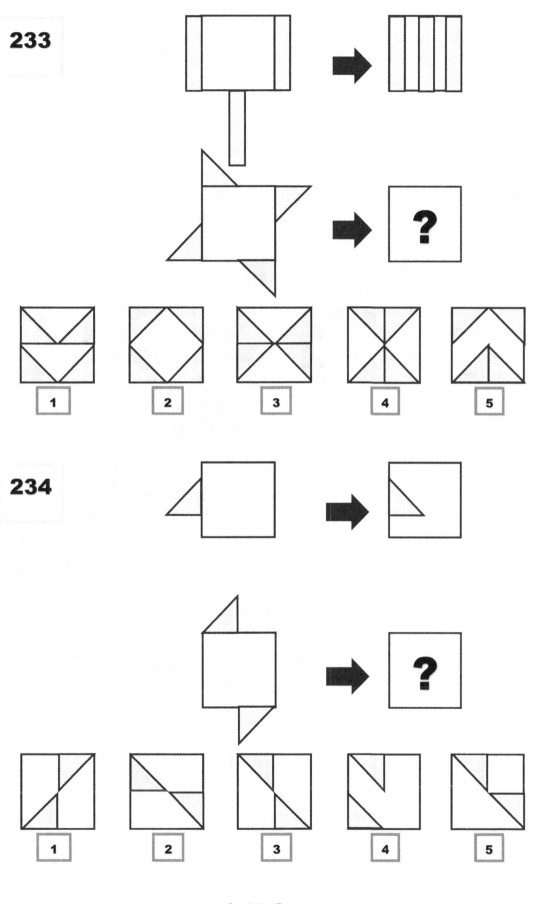

233

234

235

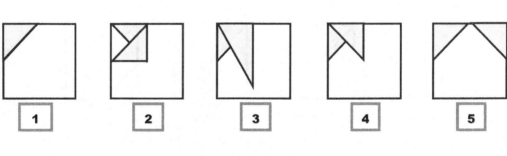

236

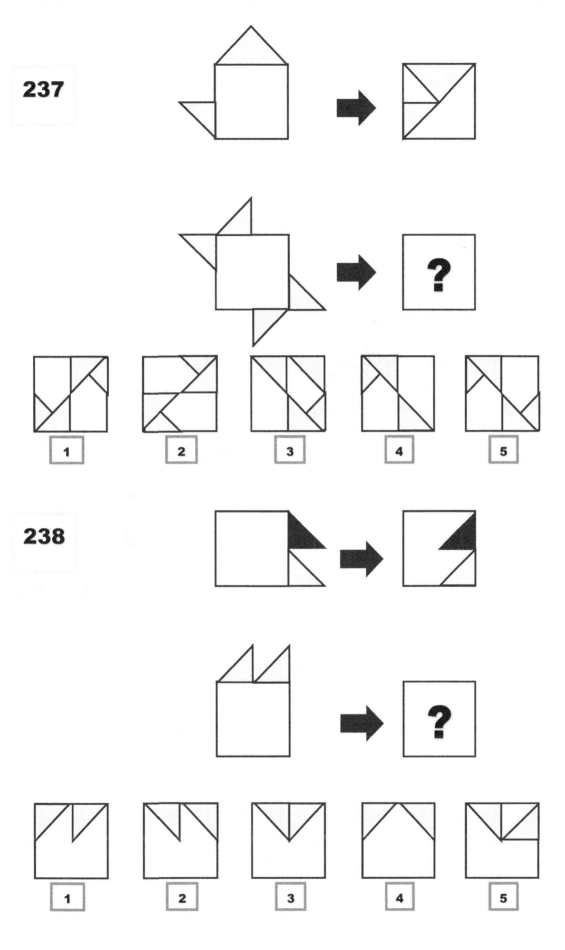

237

238

239

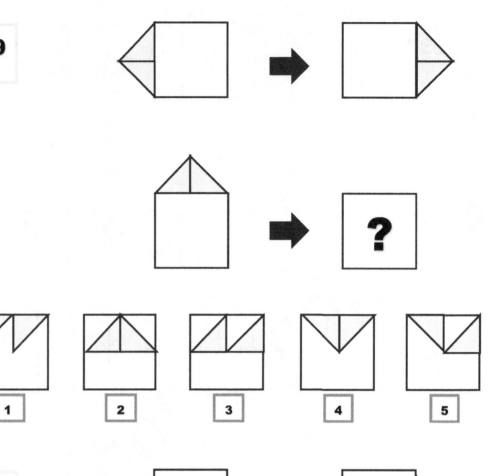

240

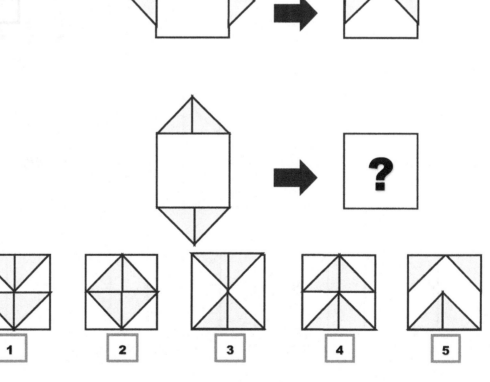

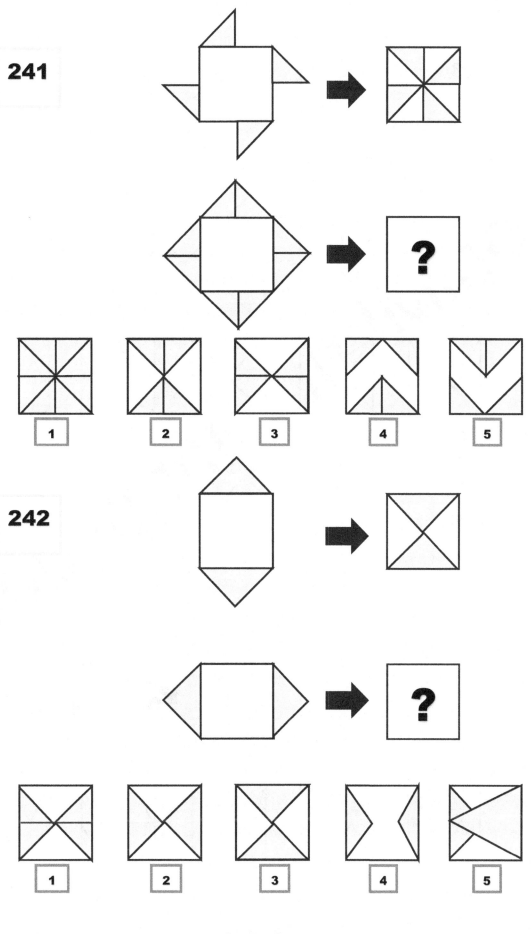

241

242

243

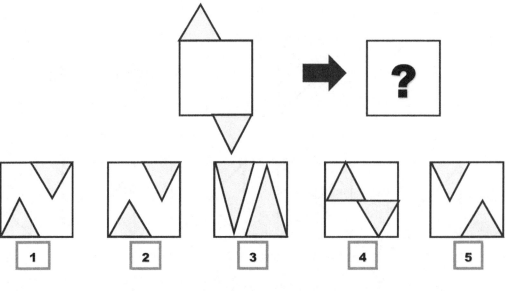

244

245

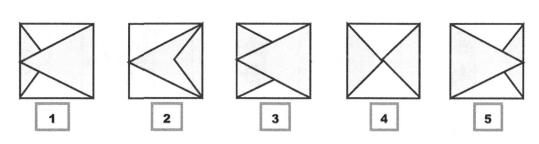

246

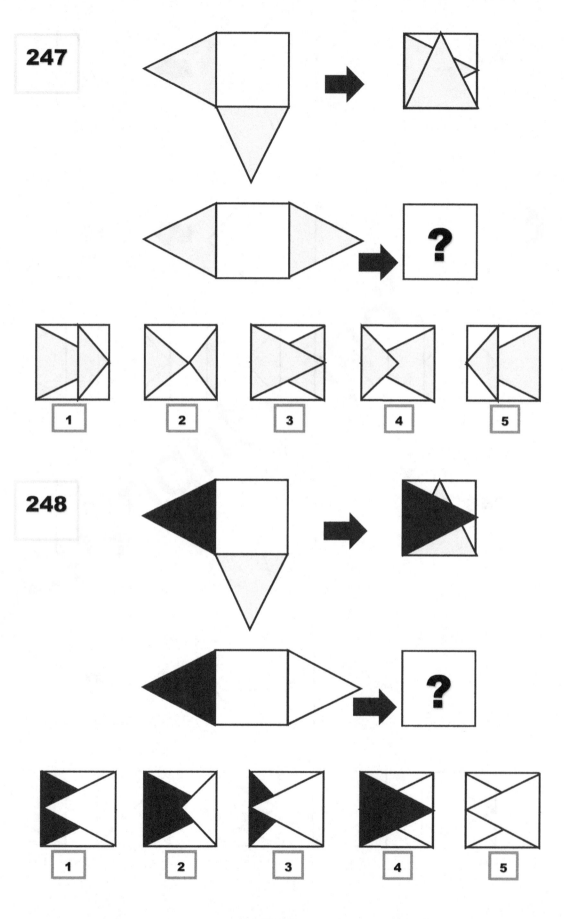

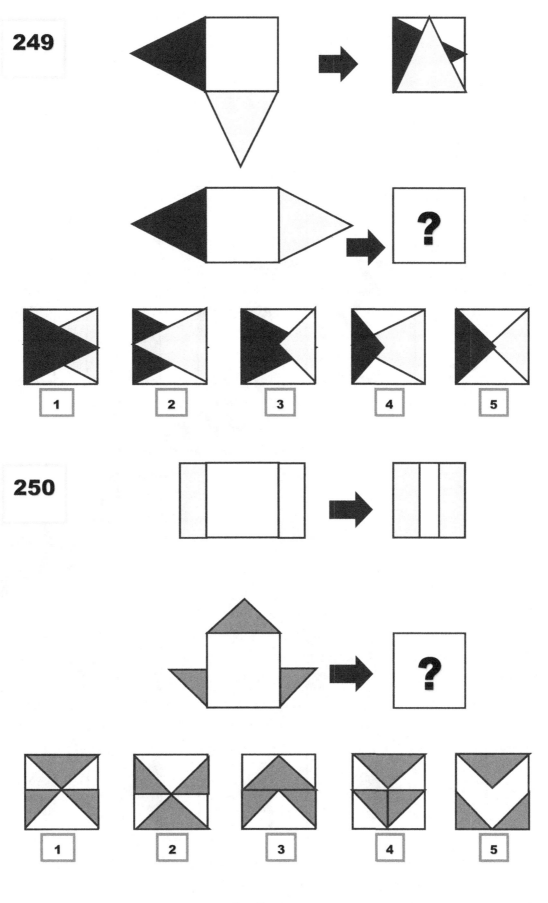

251

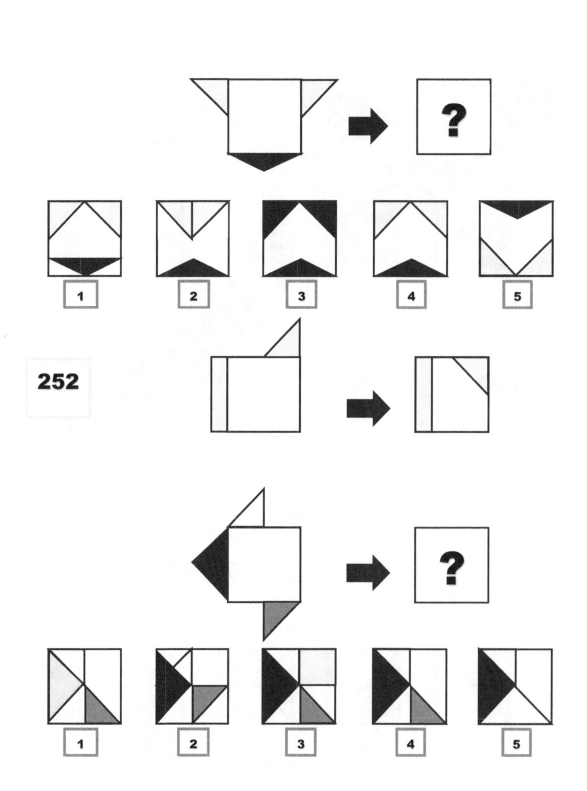

253

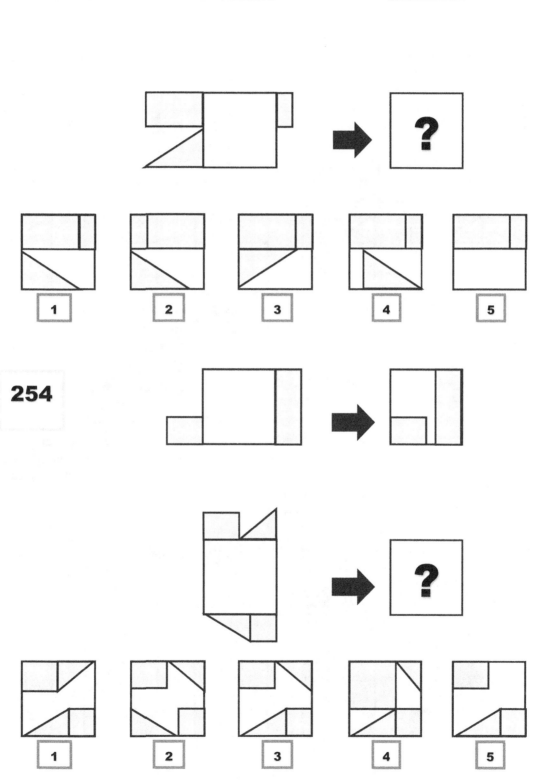

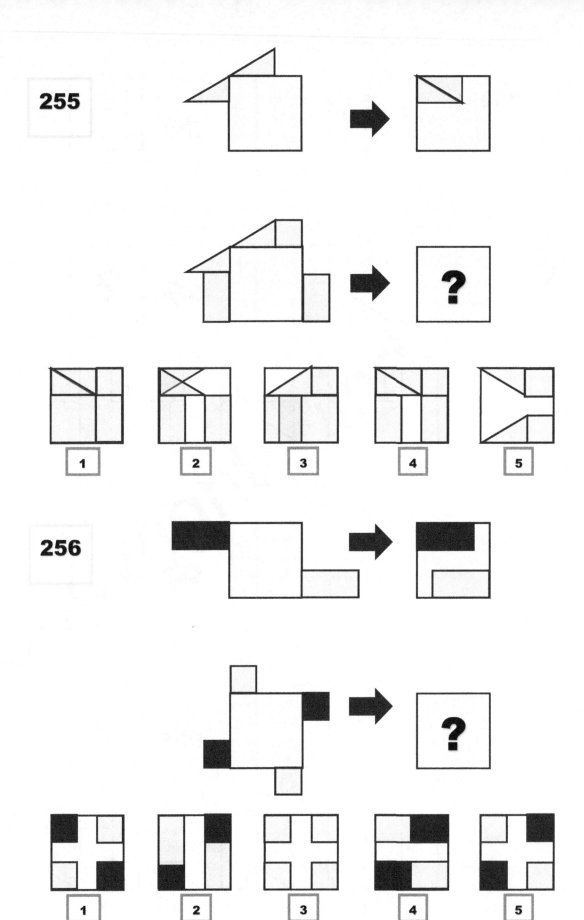

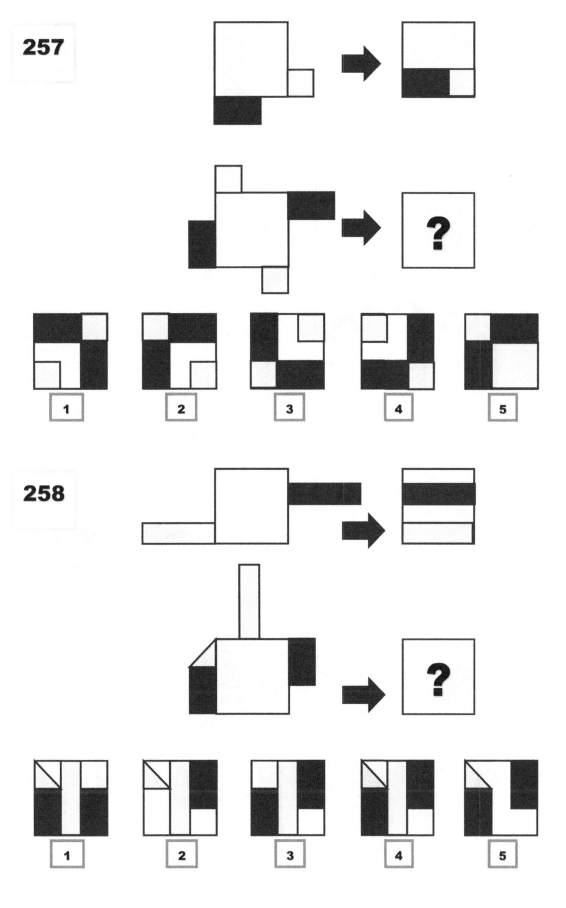

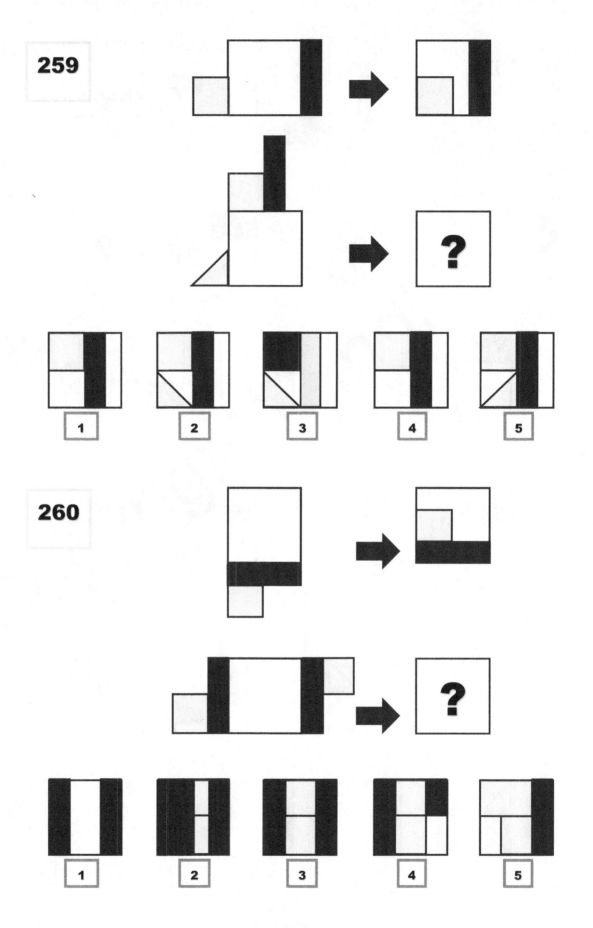

261

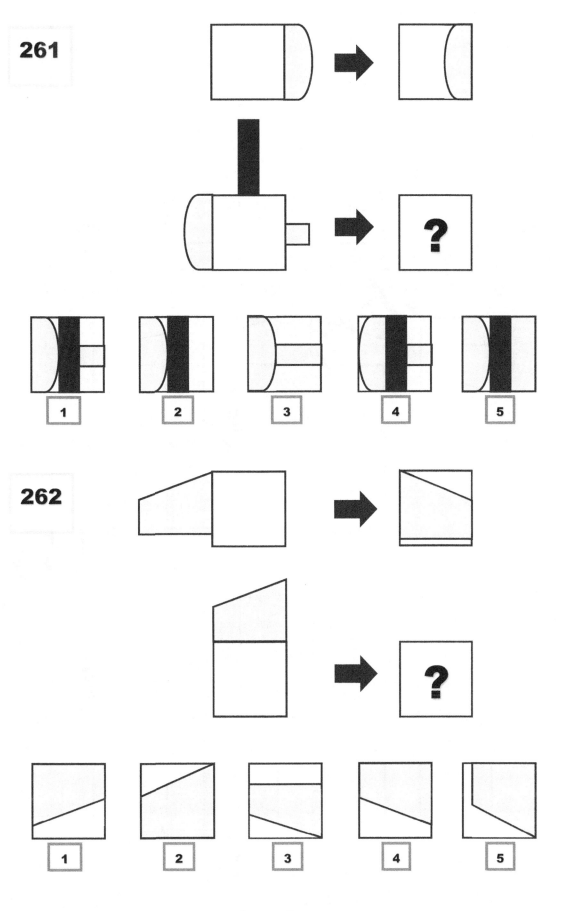

262

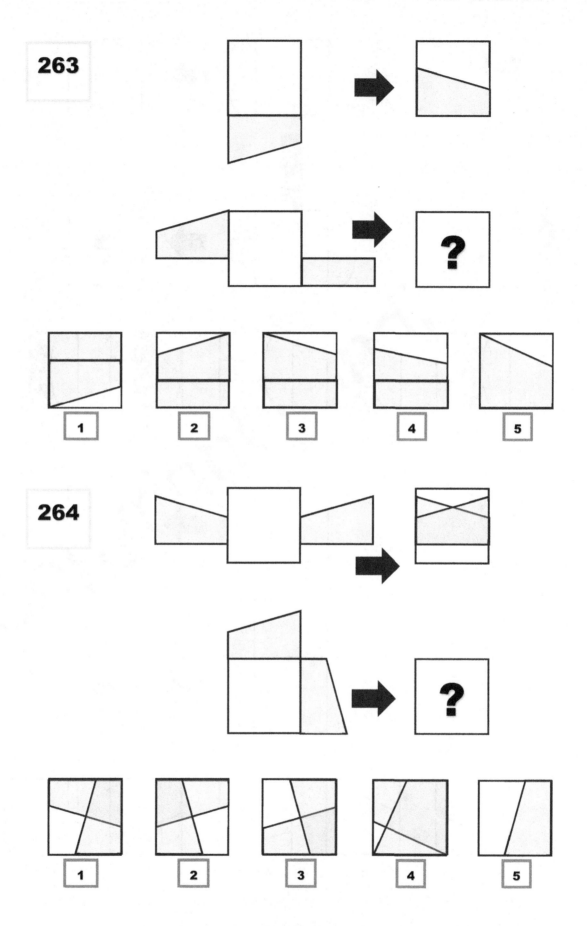

263

264

174

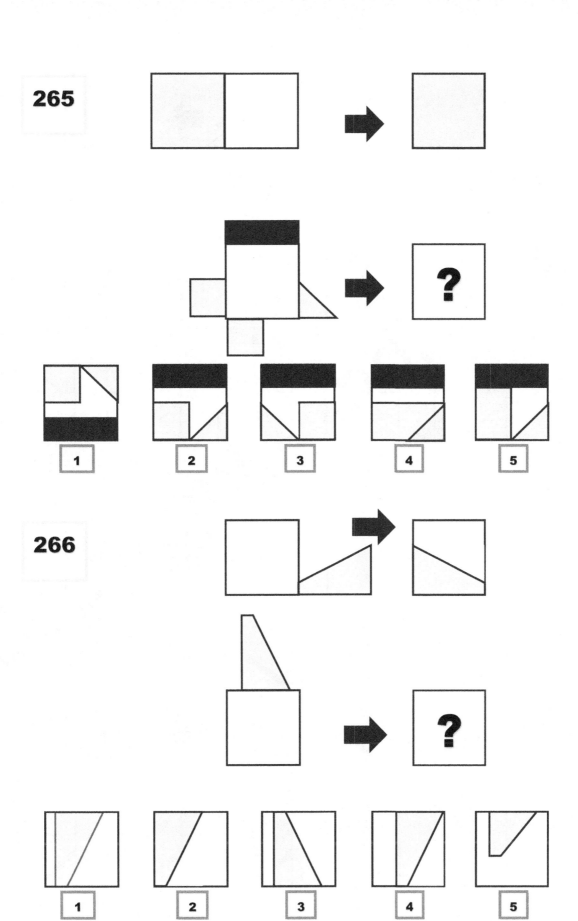

265

266

267

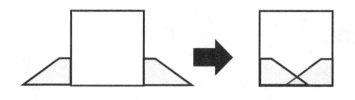

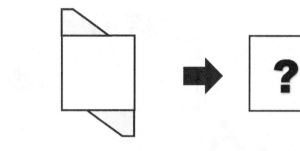

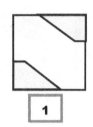  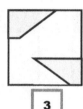 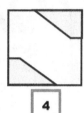 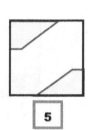

1   2   3   4   5

268

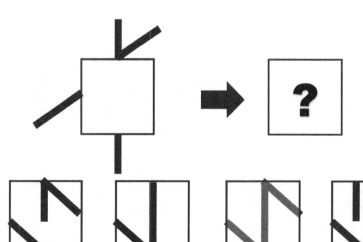

1   2   3   4   5

269

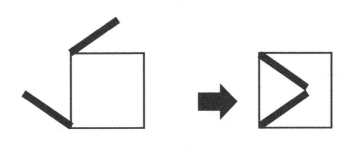

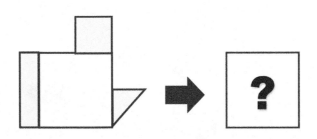

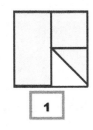 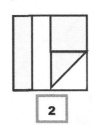 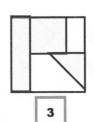 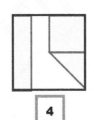 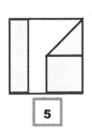

270

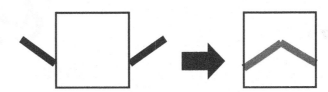

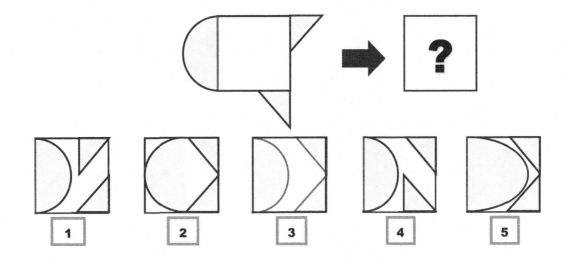

271

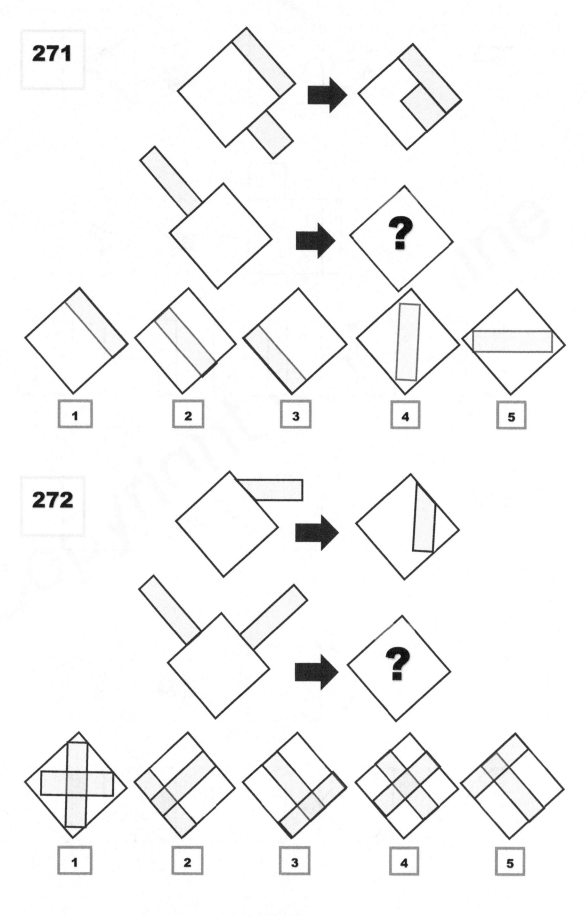

272

178

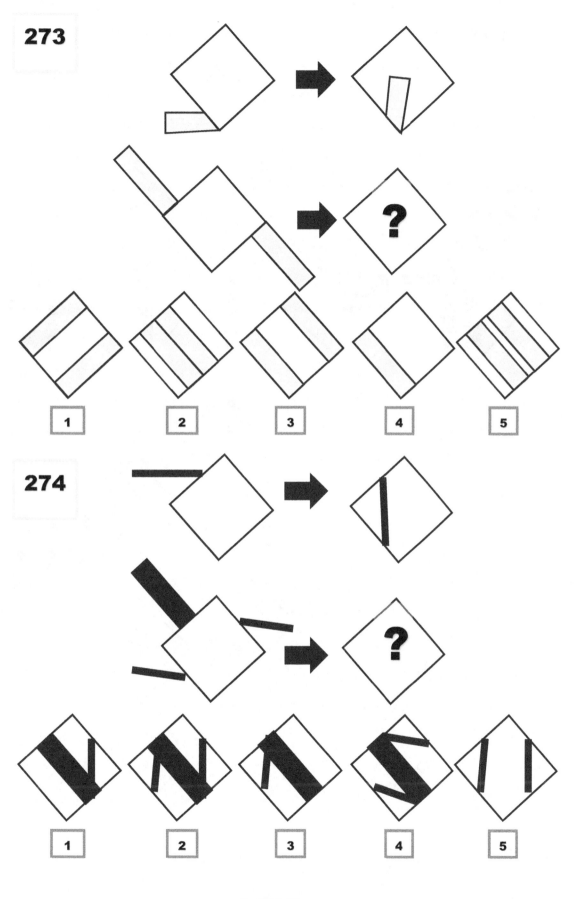

273

274

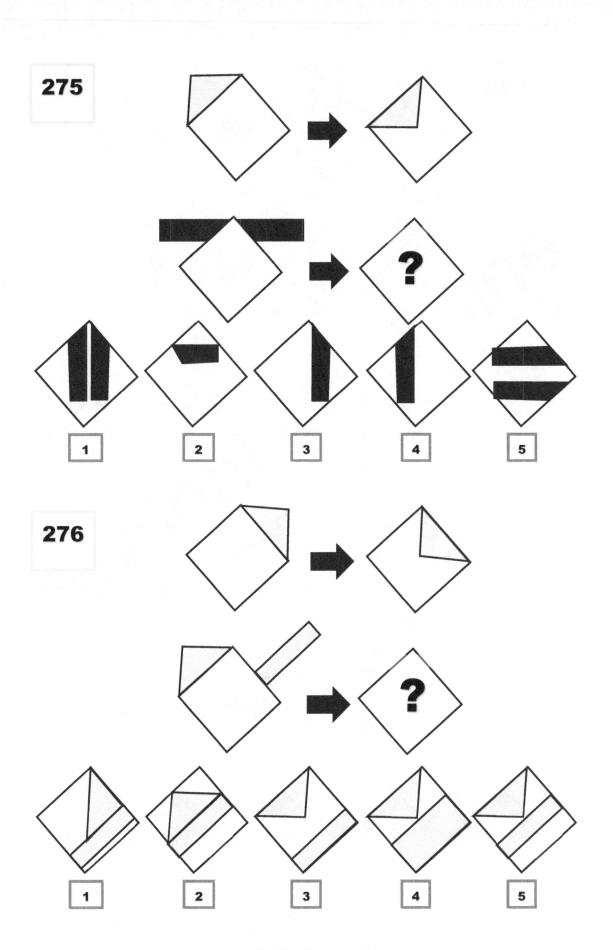

275

276

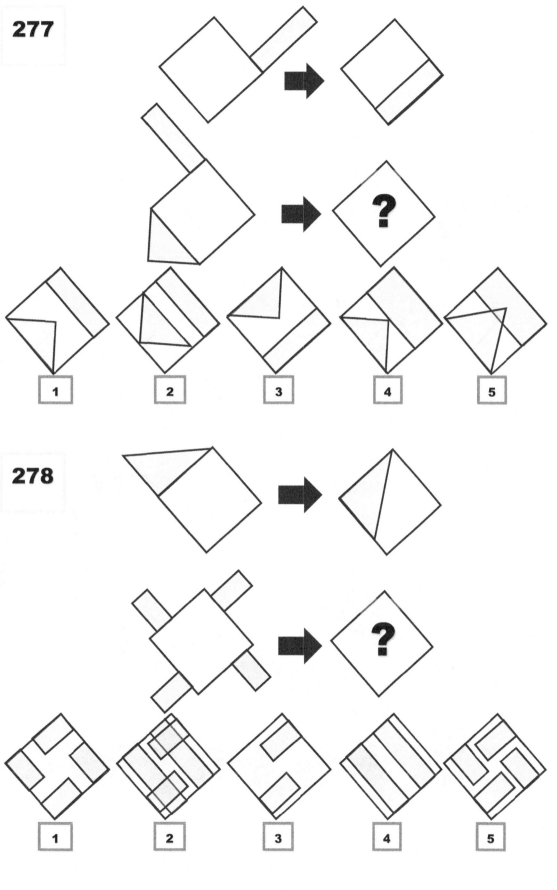

281

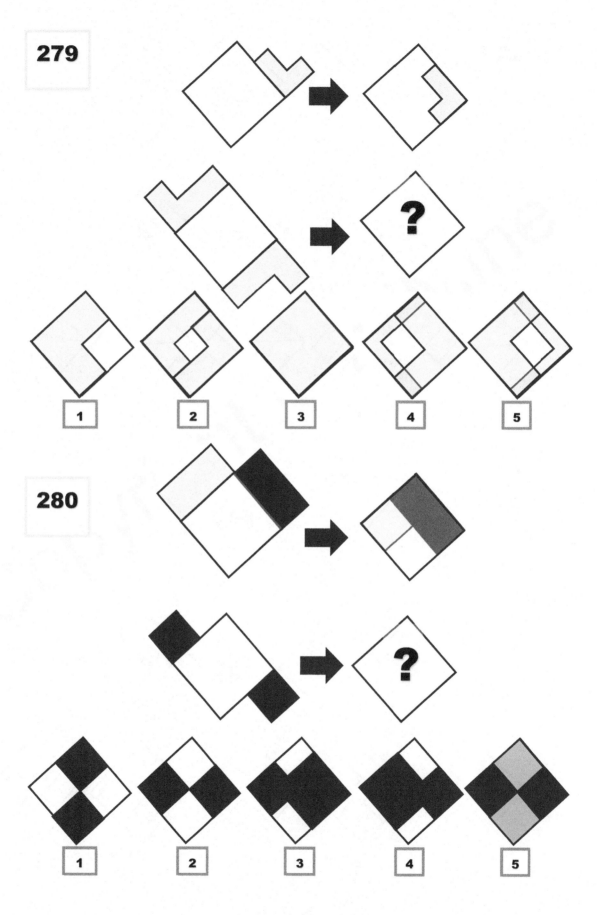

279

280

182

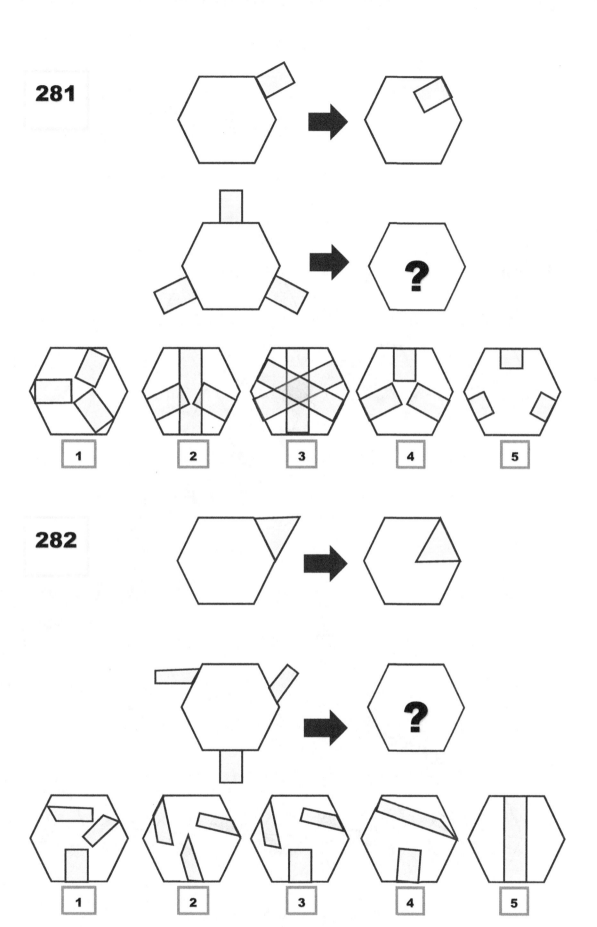

281

282

183

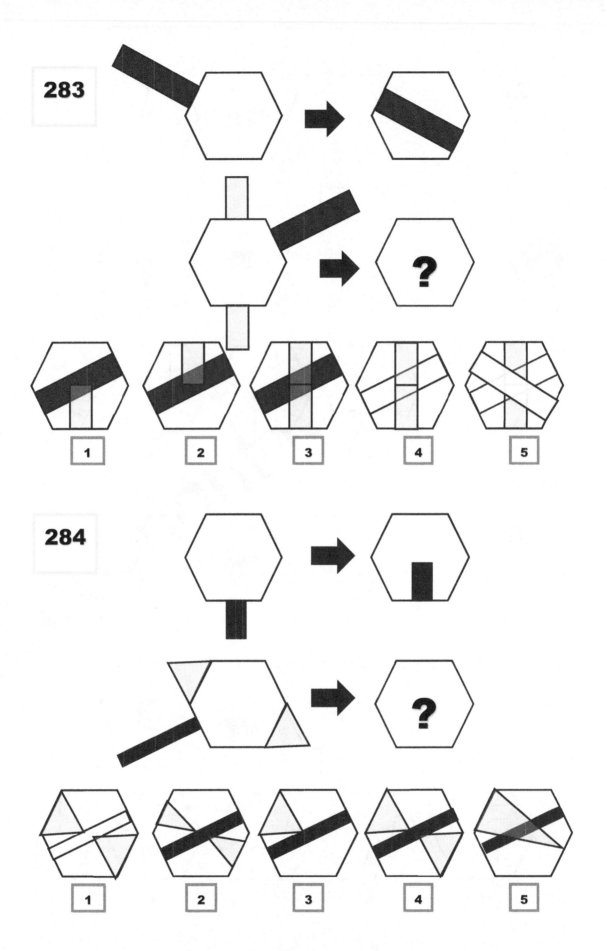

285

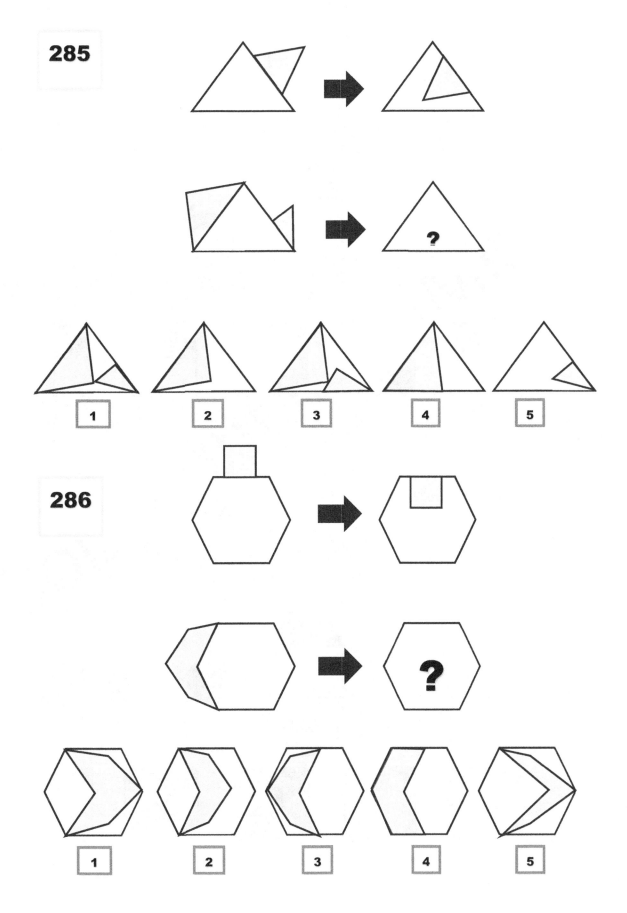

286

185

287

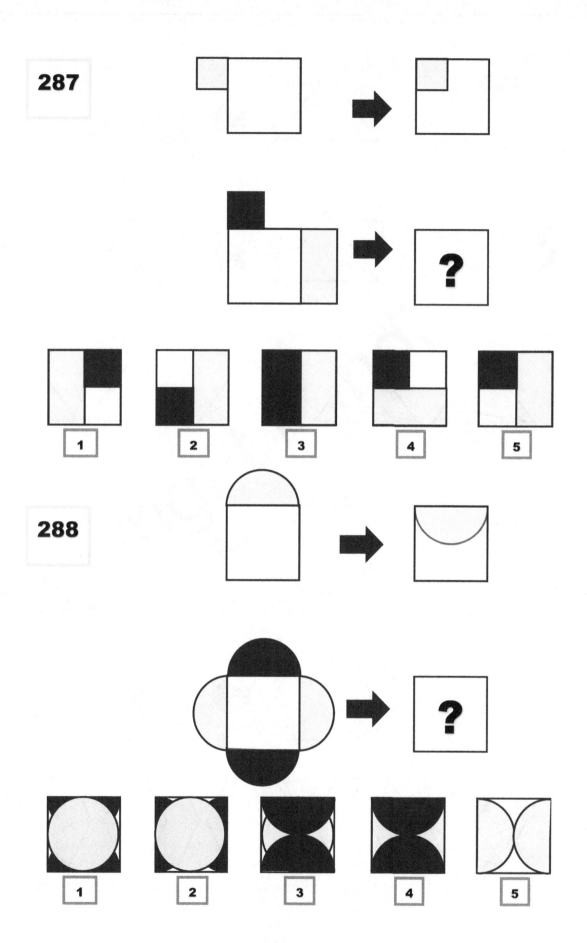

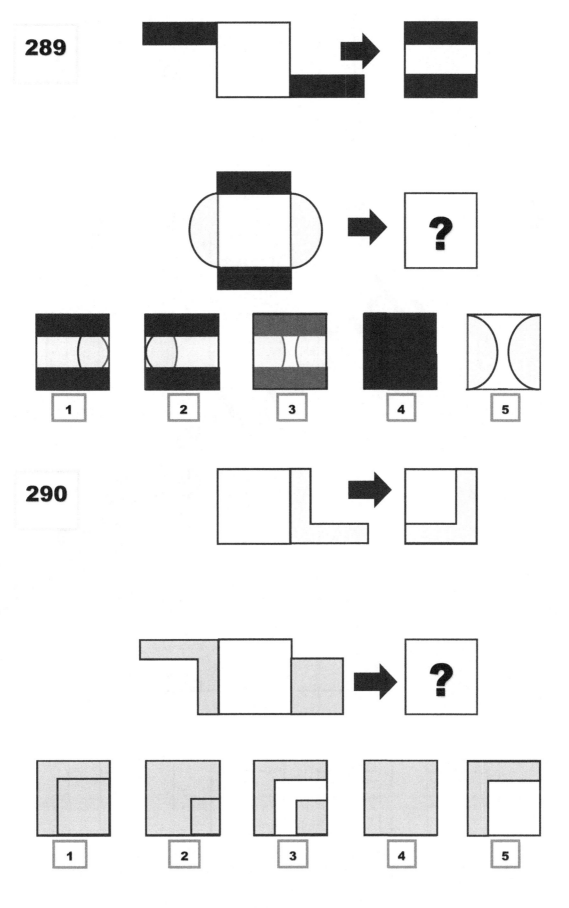

289

290

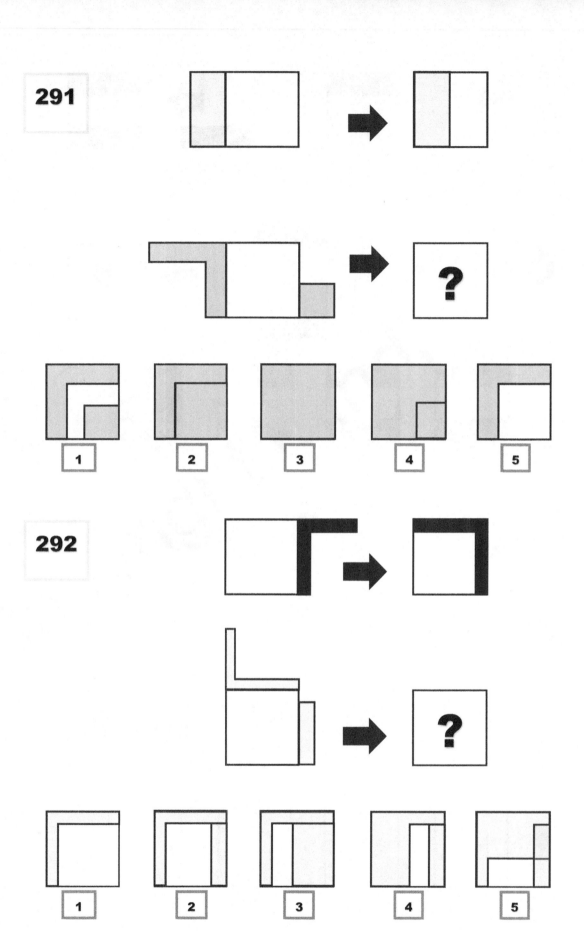

291

292

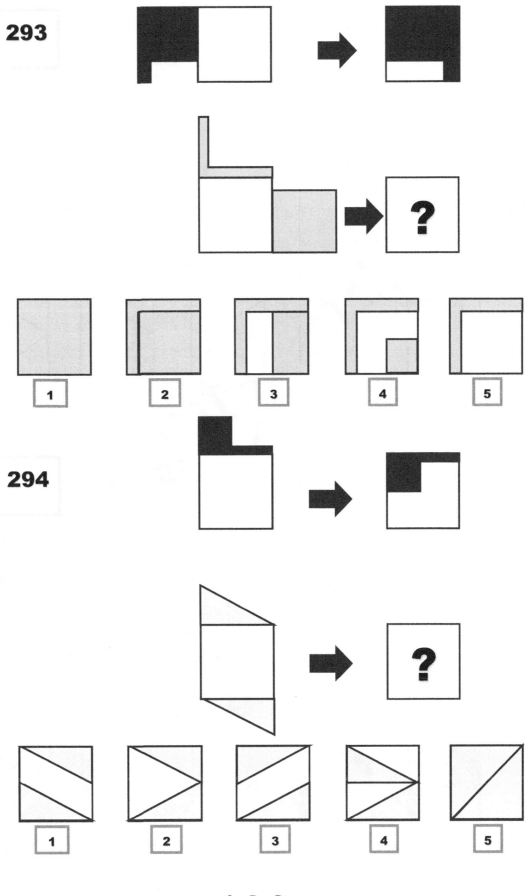

189

295

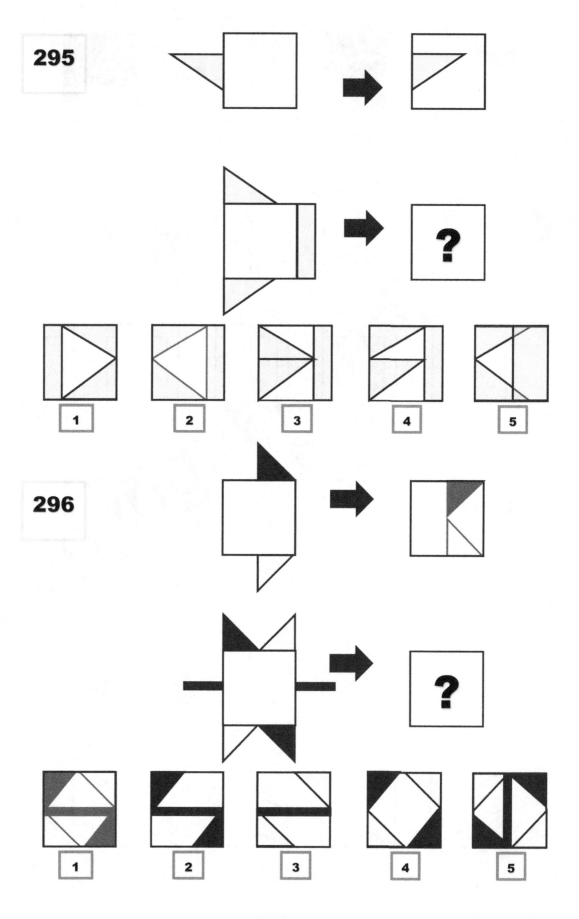

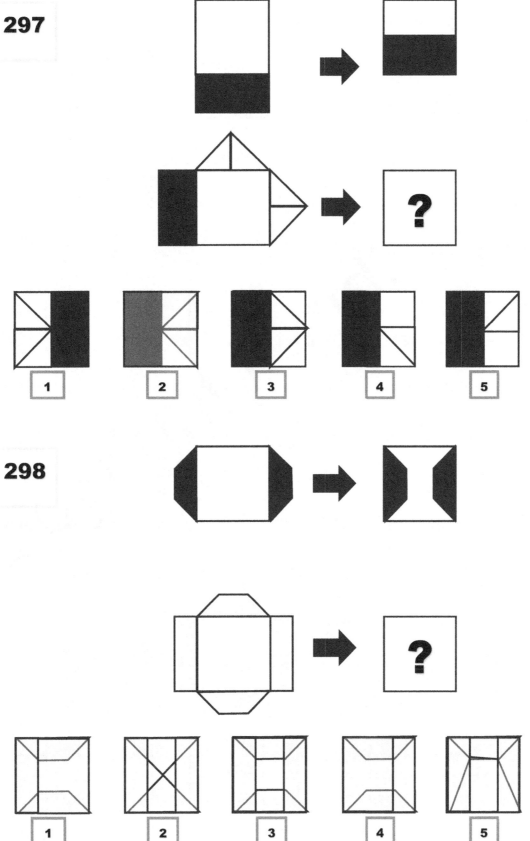

297

298

191

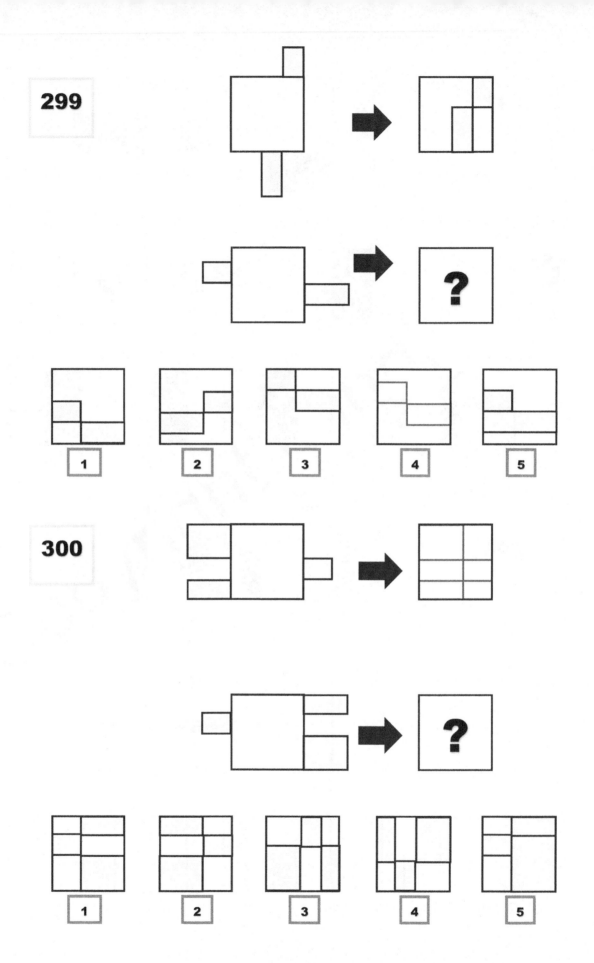

299

300

Full Length
PRACTICE TEST - 1

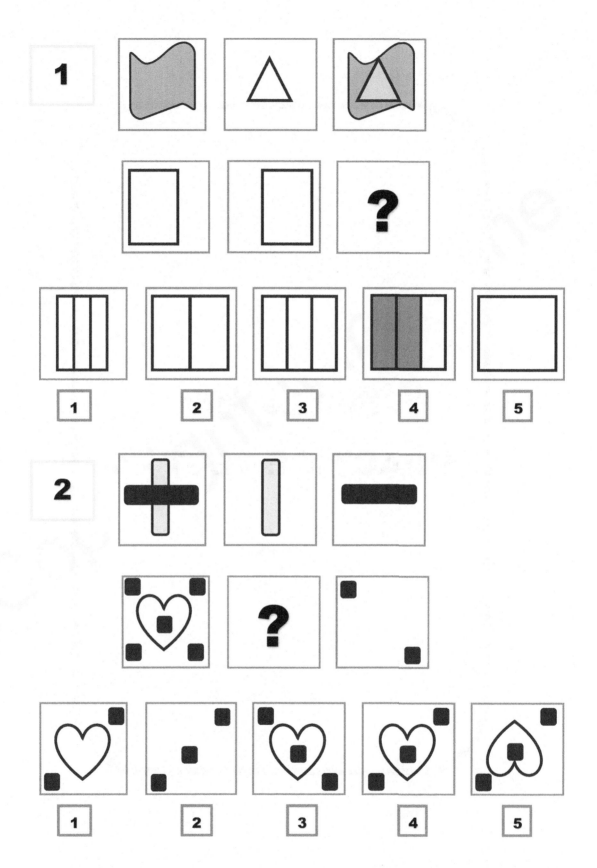

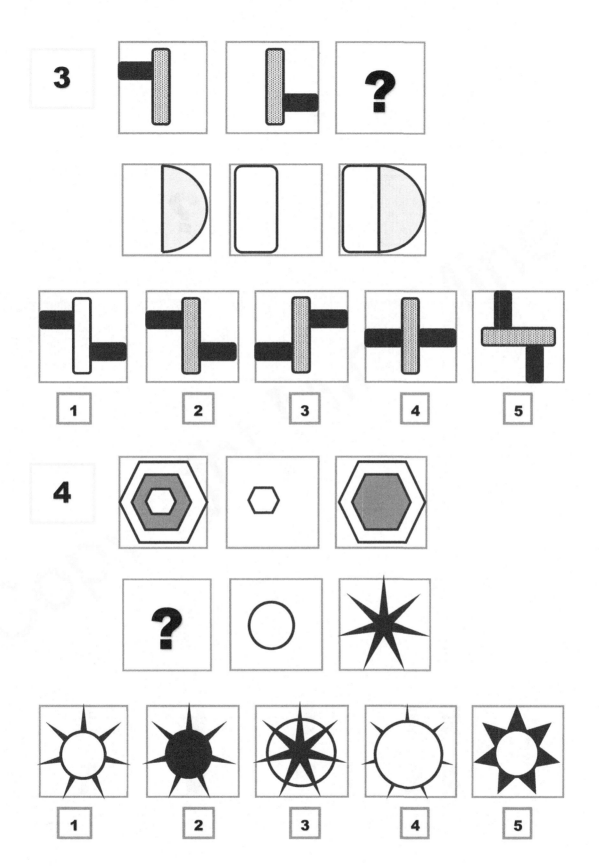

195

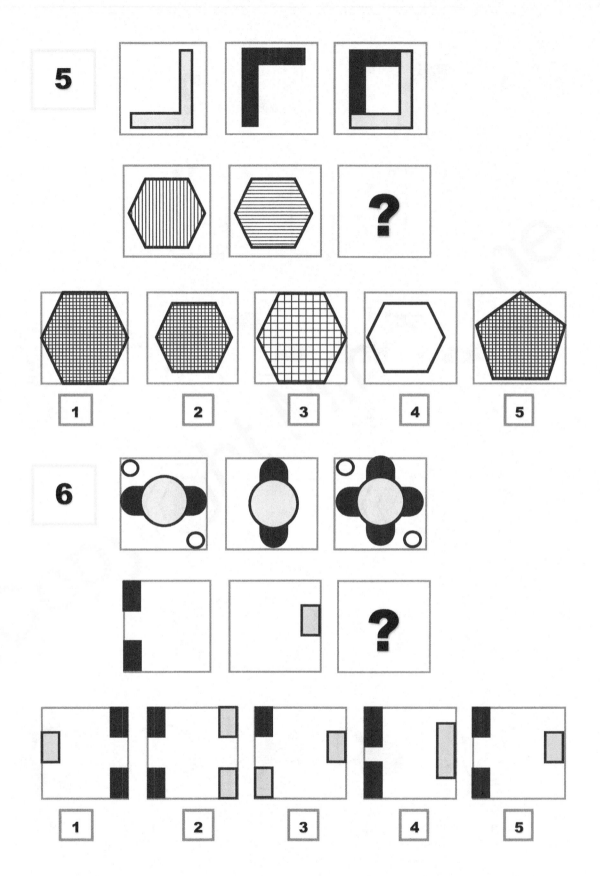

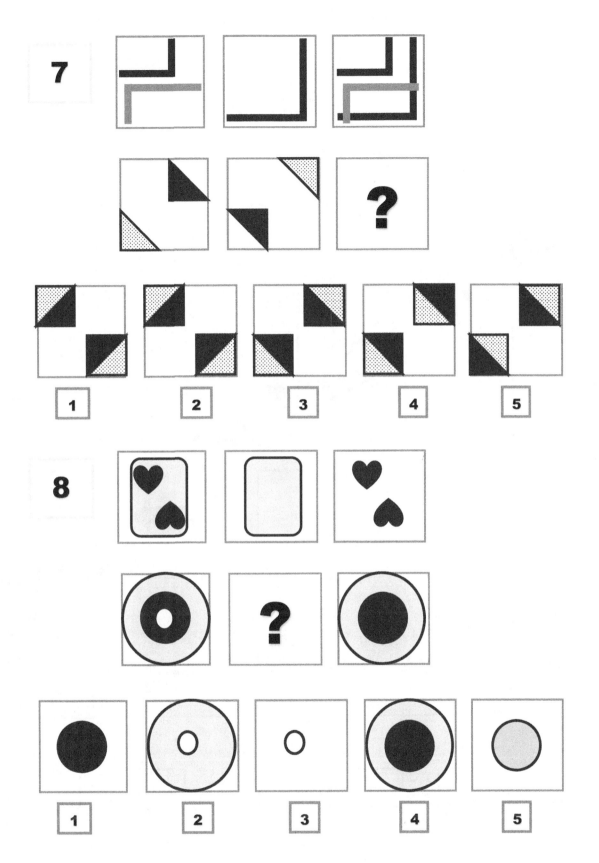

9

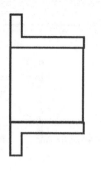 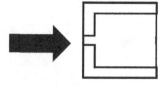

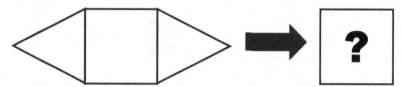

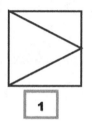 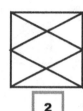 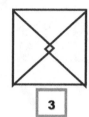 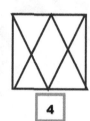 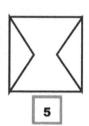

| 1 | 2 | 3 | 4 | 5 |

10

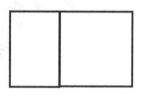

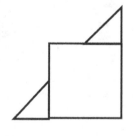

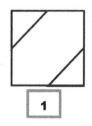  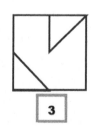 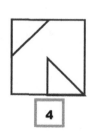 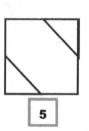

| 1 | 2 | 3 | 4 | 5 |

11

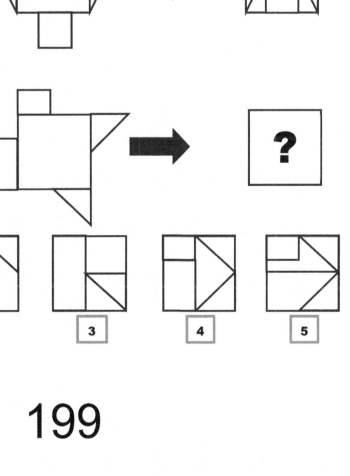

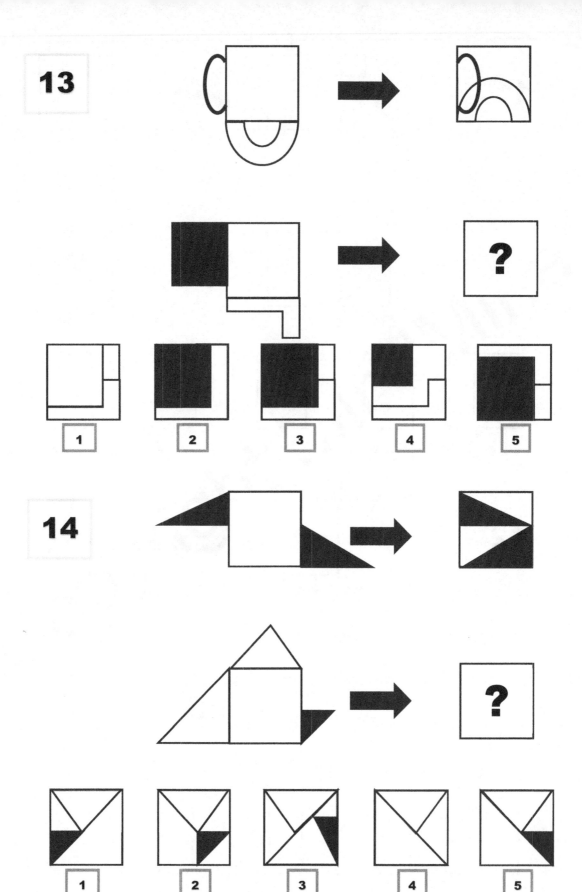

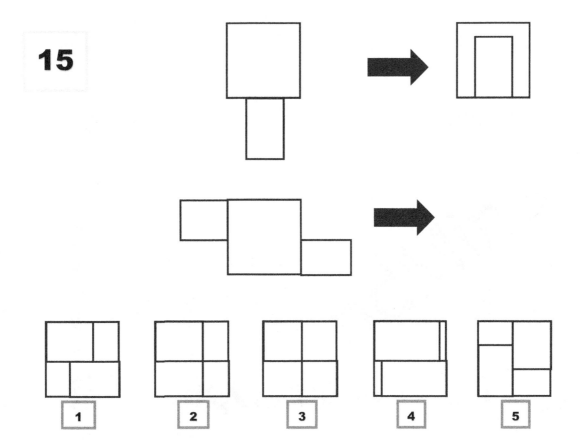

Full Length

PRACTICE TEST - 2

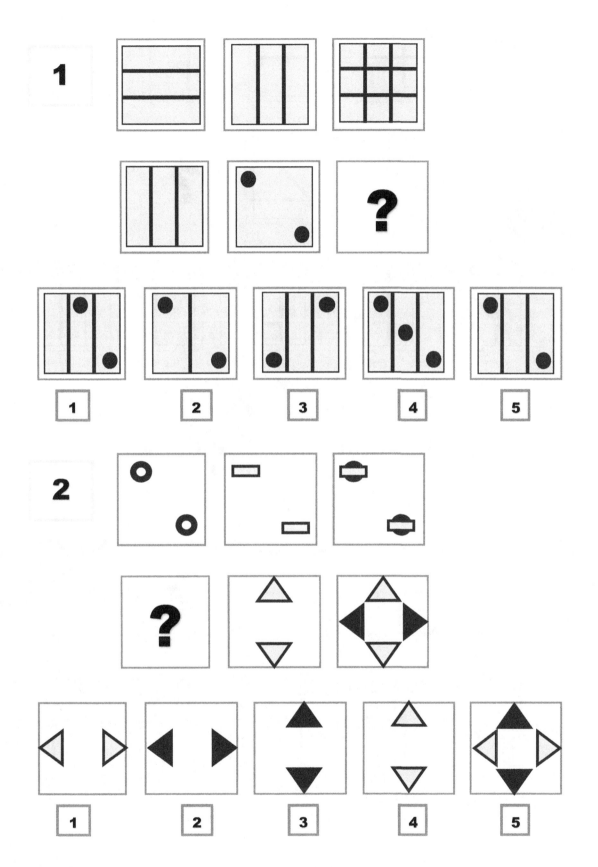

203

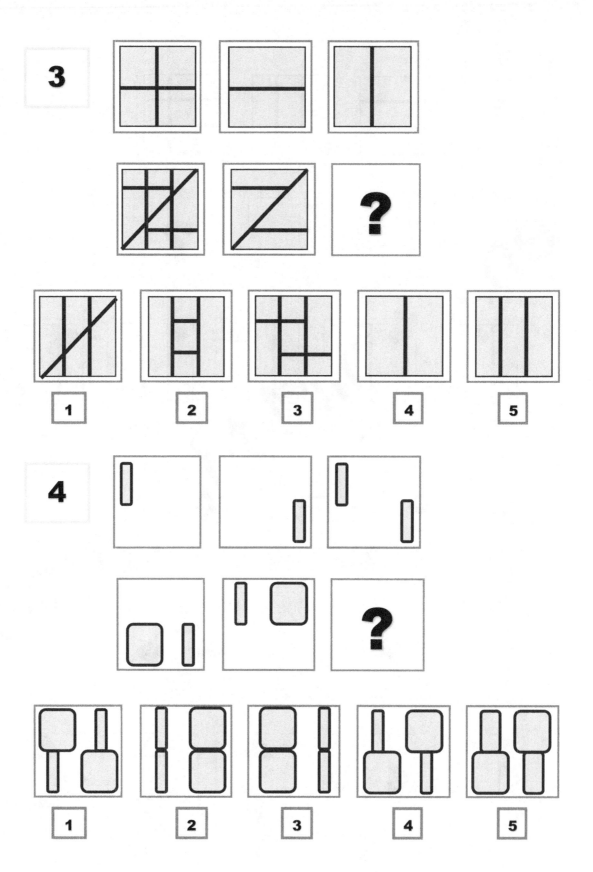

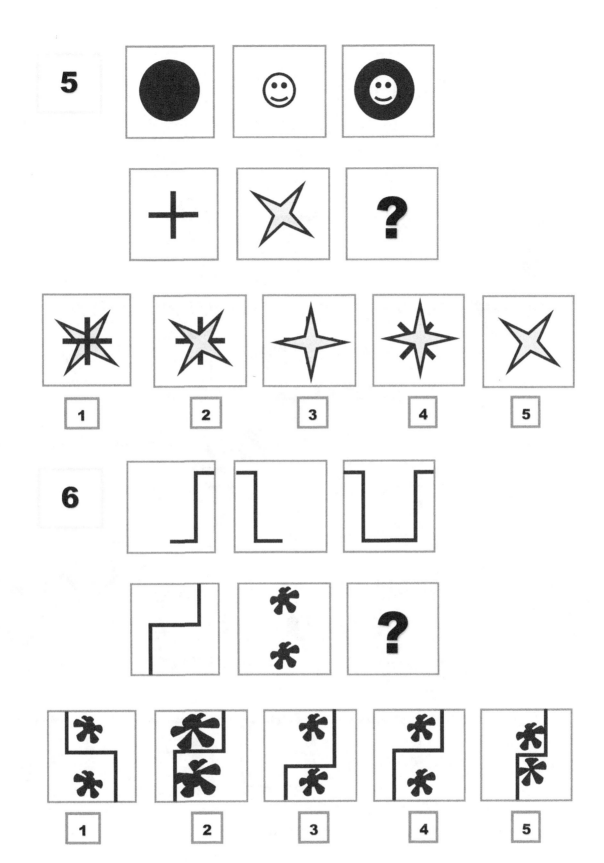

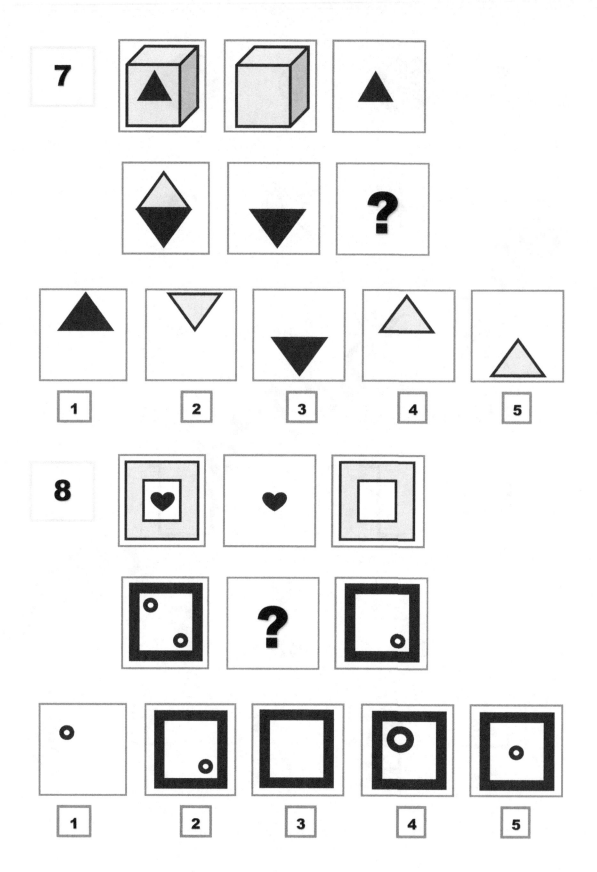

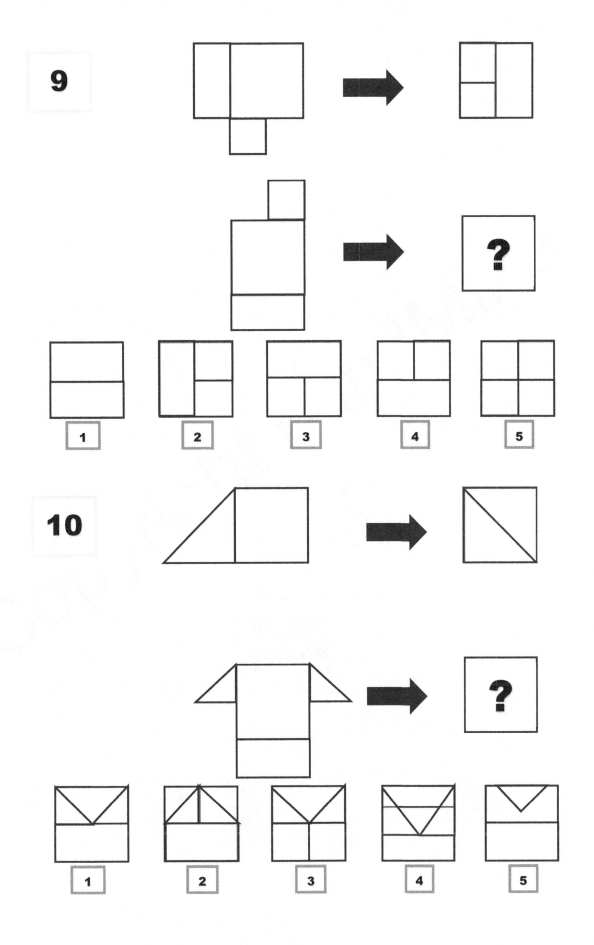

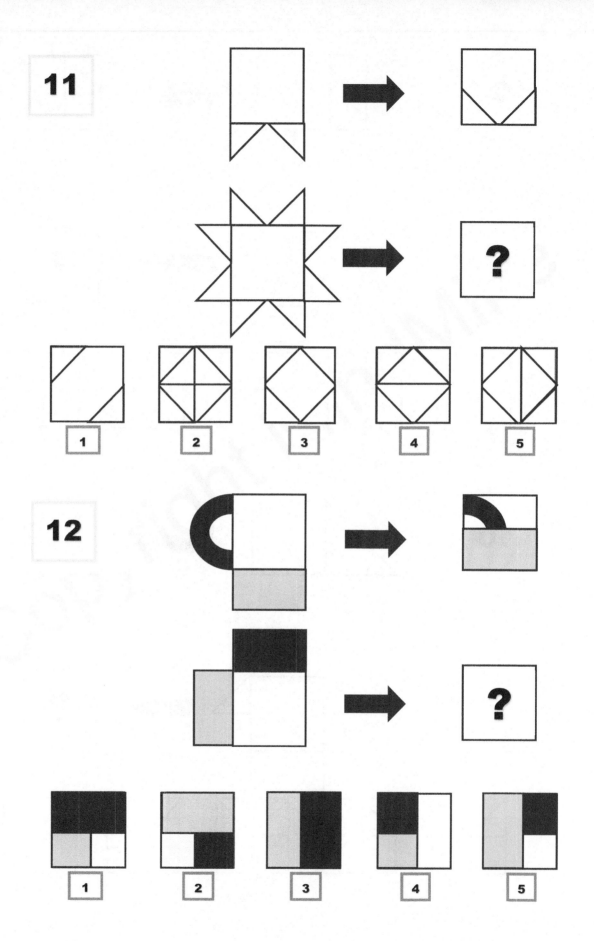

13

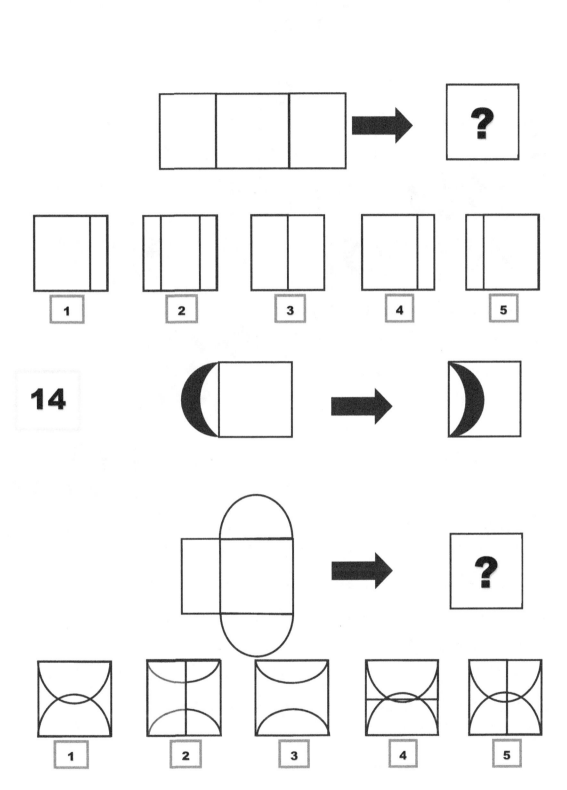

15

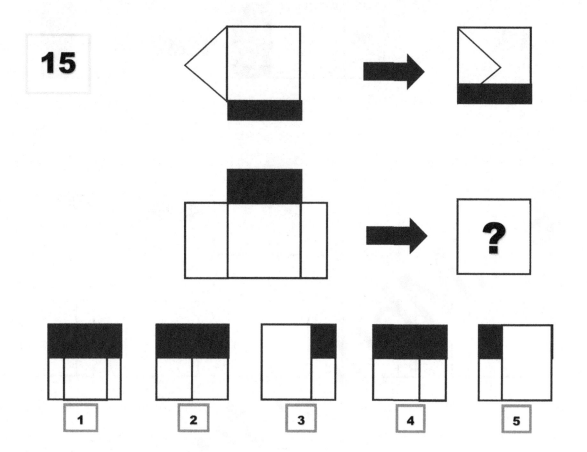

ANSWERS

ANSWERS TO NNAT QUESTIONS

QUESTION #	ANSWER	ANALOGY
1	3	Add Figures
2	2	Add Figures
3	5	Add Figures
4	4	Add Figures
5	1	Add Figures
6	2	Add Figures
7	1	Add Figures
8	1	Add Figures
9	1	Add Figures
10	1	Add Figures
11	2	Add Figures
12	5	Add Figures
13	4	Add Figures
14	2	Add Figures
15	3	Add Figures
16	1	Add Figures
17	3	Add Figures
18	5	Add Figures
19	1	Add Figures
20	2	Add Figures
21	3	Add Figures
22	4	Add Figures
23	1	Add Figures
24	5	Add Figures
25	3	Add Figures
26	2	Add Figures
27	3	Add Figures
28	2	Add Figures

ANSWERS TO NNAT QUESTIONS

QUESTION #	ANSWER	ANALOGY
29	5	Add Figures
30	1	Add Figures
31	5	Add Figures
32	4	Add Figures
33	2	Add Figures
34	5	Add Figures
35	2	Add Figures
36	4	Add Figures
37	4	Add Figures
38	1	Add Figures
39	2	Add Figures
40	4	Add Figures
41	5	Add Figures
42	3	Add Figures
43	3	Add Figures
44	3	Add Figures
45	3	Add Figures
46	5	Add Figures
47	3	Add Figures
48	4	Add Figures
49	1	Add Figures
50	3	Add Figures
51	4	Add Figures
52	3	Add Figures
53	2	Add Figures
54	2	Add Figures
55	3	Add Figures
56	3	Add Figures

ANSWERS TO NNAT QUESTIONS

QUESTION #	ANSWER	ANALOGY
57	2	Add Figures
58	4	Add Figures
59	2	Add Figures
60	3	Add Figures
61	4	Add Figures
62	1	Add Figures
63	2	Add Figures
64	5	Add Figures
65	3	Add Figures
66	4	Add Figures
67	2	Add Figures
68	3	Add Figures
69	3	Add Figures
70	4	Add Figures
71	2	Add Figures
72	1	Add Figures
73	5	Add Figures
74	1	Add Figures
75	2	Add Figures
76	5	Add Figures
77	2	Add Figures
78	5	Add Figures
79	1	Add Figures
80	3	Add Figures
81	5	Add Figures
82	4	Add Figures
83	1	Add Figures
84	2	Add Figures

ANSWERS TO NNAT QUESTIONS

QUESTION #	ANSWER	ANALOGY
85	4	Add Figures
86	2	Add Figures
87	2	Add Figures
88	5	Add Figures
89	3	Add Figures
90	3	Add Figures
91	1	Add Figures
92	3	Add Figures
93	4	Add Figures
94	2	Add Figures
95	3	Add Figures
96	2	Add Figures
97	1	Add Figures
98	3	Add Figures
99	3	Add Figures
100	5	Add Figures
101	3	Subtract Figures
102	4	Subtract Figures
103	5	Subtract Figures
104	2	Subtract Figures
105	4	Subtract Figures
106	3	Subtract Figures
107	2	Subtract Figures
108	1	Subtract Figures
109	4	Subtract Figures
110	4	Subtract Figures
111	1	Subtract Figures

ANSWERS TO NNAT QUESTIONS

QUESTION #	ANSWER	ANALOGY
112	3	Subtract Figures
113	1	Subtract Figures
114	2	Subtract Figures
115	2	Subtract Figures
116	5	Subtract Figures
117	3	Subtract Figures
118	2	Subtract Figures
119	5	Subtract Figures
120	3	Subtract Figures
121	3	Subtract Figures
122	3	Subtract Figures
123	1	Subtract Figures
124	4	Subtract Figures
125	5	Subtract Figures
126	1	Subtract Figures
127	4	Subtract Figures
128	2	Subtract Figures
129	3	Subtract Figures
130	3	Subtract Figures
131	5	Subtract Figures
132	3	Subtract Figures
133	3	Subtract Figures
134	3	Subtract Figures
135	5	Subtract Figures
136	1	Subtract Figures
137	1	Subtract Figures
138	2	Subtract Figures
139	5	Subtract Figures

ANSWERS TO NNAT QUESTIONS

QUESTION #	ANSWER	ANALOGY
140	3	Subtract Figures
141	3	Subtract Figures
142	3	Subtract Figures
143	5	Subtract Figures
144	4	Subtract Figures
145	3	Subtract Figures
146	4	Subtract Figures
147	3	Subtract Figures
148	1	Subtract Figures
149	2	Subtract Figures
150	3	Subtract Figures
151	4	Subtract Figures
152	4	Subtract Figures
153	5	Subtract Figures
154	3	Subtract Figures
155	2	Subtract Figures
156	2	Subtract Figures
157	4	Subtract Figures
158	1	Subtract Figures
159	2	Subtract Figures
160	5	Subtract Figures
161	4	Subtract Figures
162	3	Subtract Figures
163	1	Subtract Figures
164	3	Subtract Figures
165	5	Subtract Figures
166	3	Subtract Figures
167	2	Subtract Figures

ANSWERS TO NNAT QUESTIONS

QUESTION #	ANSWER	ANALOGY
168	1	Subtract Figures
169	3	Subtract Figures
170	2	Subtract Figures
171	5	Subtract Figures
172	3	Subtract Figures
173	3	Subtract Figures
174	4	Subtract Figures
175	3	Subtract Figures
176	3	Subtract Figures
177	2	Subtract Figures
178	4	Subtract Figures
179	3	Subtract Figures
180	5	Subtract Figures
181	2	Subtract Figures
182	3	Subtract Figures
183	5	Subtract Figures
184	2	Subtract Figures
185	2	Subtract Figures
186	3	Subtract Figures
187	4	Subtract Figures
188	3	Subtract Figures
189	3	Subtract Figures
190	4	Subtract Figures
191	2	Subtract Figures
192	1	Subtract Figures
193	4	Subtract Figures
194	2	Subtract Figures
195	4	Subtract Figures

ANSWERS TO NNAT QUESTIONS

QUESTION #	ANSWER	ANALOGY
196	3	Subtract Figures
197	5	Subtract Figures
198	4	Subtract Figures
199	1	Subtract Figures
200	1	Subtract Figures
201	4	Fold Figures
202	3	Fold Figures
203	2	Fold Figures
204	1	Fold Figures
205	4	Fold Figures
206	2	Fold Figures
207	1	Fold Figures
208	2	Fold Figures
209	1	Fold Figures
210	5	Fold Figures
211	3	Fold Figures
212	5	Fold Figures
213	1	Fold Figures
214	4	Fold Figures
215	3	Fold Figures
216	2	Fold Figures
217	2	Fold Figures
218	4	Fold Figures
219	1	Fold Figures
220	5	Fold Figures
221	2	Fold Figures
222	4	Fold Figures

ANSWERS TO NNAT QUESTIONS

QUESTION #	ANSWER	ANALOGY
223	3	Fold Figures
224	2	Fold Figures
225	5	Fold Figures
226	4	Fold Figures
227	2	Fold Figures
228	5	Fold Figures
229	3	Fold Figures
230	2	Fold Figures
231	2	Fold Figures
232	1	Fold Figures
233	2	Fold Figures
234	3	Fold Figures
235	4	Fold Figures
236	4	Fold Figures
237	5	Fold Figures
238	2	Fold Figures
239	4	Fold Figures
240	3	Fold Figures
241	1	Fold Figures
242	2	Fold Figures
243	3	Fold Figures
244	5	Fold Figures
245	3	Fold Figures
246	5	Fold Figures
247	3	Fold Figures
248	4	Fold Figures
249	2	Fold Figures
250	1	Fold Figures

ANSWERS TO NNAT QUESTIONS

QUESTION #	ANSWER	ANALOGY
251	4	Fold Figures
252	4	Fold Figures
253	1	Fold Figures
254	3	Fold Figures
255	4	Fold Figures
256	5	Fold Figures
257	2	Fold Figures
258	4	Fold Figures
259	2	Fold Figures
260	3	Fold Figures
261	1	Fold Figures
262	4	Fold Figures
263	3	Fold Figures
264	1	Fold Figures
265	2	Fold Figures
266	1	Fold Figures
267	5	Fold Figures
268	4	Fold Figures
269	4	Fold Figures
270	3	Fold Figures
271	2	Fold Figures
272	4	Fold Figures
273	3	Fold Figures
274	2	Fold Figures
275	1	Fold Figures
276	5	Fold Figures
277	1	Fold Figures
278	5	Fold Figures

ANSWERS TO NNAT QUESTIONS

QUESTION #	ANSWER	ANALOGY
279	2	Fold Figures
280	2	Fold Figures
281	4	Fold Figures
282	3	Fold Figures
283	3	Fold Figures
284	4	Fold Figures
285	1	Fold Figures
286	2	Fold Figures
287	5	Fold Figures
288	4	Fold Figures
289	3	Fold Figures
290	1	Fold Figures
291	1	Fold Figures
292	2	Fold Figures
293	2	Fold Figures
294	3	Fold Figures
295	2	Fold Figures
296	1	Fold Figures
297	2	Fold Figures
298	3	Fold Figures
299	4	Fold Figures
300	1	Fold Figures

FULL LENGTH PRACTICE TEST # 1
ANSWERS

QUESTION #	ANSWER	ANALOGY
1	3	Add Figures
2	4	Subtract 3rd figure from 1st figure to get 2nd figure
3	2	Add Figures
4	1	Add 2nd & 3rd Figures to get 1st one.
5	2	Add Figures
6	5	Add Figures
7	3	Add Figures
8	3	Subtract 3rd figure from 1st figure to get 2nd figure
9	2	Fold Figures. Pay attention to size of triangles
10	5	Fold Figures
11	2	Fold Figures
12	4	Fold Figures
13	3	Fold Figures
14	5	Fold Figures
15	1	Fold Figures. Pay attention to the size of figures

FULL LENGTH PRACTICE TEST # 2
ANSWERS

QUESTION #	ANSWER	ANALOGY
1	5	Add Figures. Pay attention to position of figures
2	2	Subtract 2nd figure from 3rd figure
3	5	Subtract 2nd figure from 1st figure
4	4	Add Figures
5	2	Place 2nd figure over 1st figure
6	4	Add Figures
7	4	Subtract Figures
8	1	Subtract 3rd figure from 1st figure
9	4	Fold Figures
10	1	Fold Figures
11	3	Fold Figures
12	5	Fold Figures
13	2	Fold Figures
14	5	Fold Figures. Pay attention to the size of semicircles.
15	4	Fold Figures. Black figure folds over the right figure.

Other ways to use this book

15 Mini Practice Tests

Questions are organized by each individual concept. Picking 15 questions randomly and solving them out of order serve as a mini practice test. **About 12 mini practice tests** can be generated.

500 Additional Questions

 After solving each question, Write down the answer in the box with **"?"**.

 Now cover first box on first row and solve question. This will generate 200 additional questions.

 Now cover 2nd box on first row and solve question. This will generate 200 additional questions.

 Now cover First box on 2nd row and solve question. This will generate 200 additional questions.

 Now cover 2nd box on 2nd row and solve question. This will generate 200 additional questions.

Note: Additional questions Do Not have answer choices.

Generated questions from original question #12:

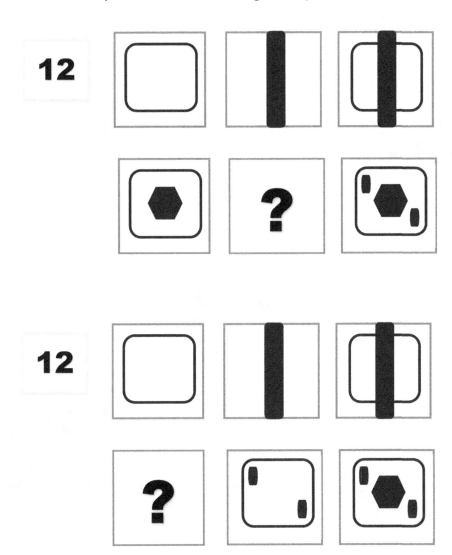

Generated questions from original question #237:

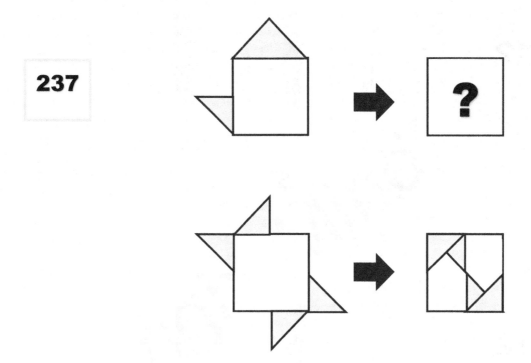

Additional Help

Have a question? You can reach author directly at

mindmineauthor@gmail.com

Made in the USA
Las Vegas, NV
14 October 2023

79092822R00129